D1489052

Streetfinder
COLOUR ATLAS & GUIDE

Contents

Legend

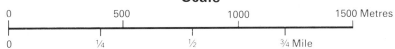

M50 — Motorway

N1 — National Primary Road

N81 — National Secondary Road

R108 — Regional Road

2 — Postal Boundaries

— Railway Station

–·–·–·– Local Authority Boundaries

Scale

```
0                500              1000            1500 Metres
0               1/4               1/2            3/4 Mile
```

Bartholomew
An Imprint of HarperCollins *Publishers*
77-85 Fulham Palace Road, Hammersmith, London W6 8JB

Copyright © Bartholomew 1996

Based upon the Ordnance Survey by permission of the Government of the Republic of Ireland.

Printed in Hong Kong

2 Dublin Route Planning Map

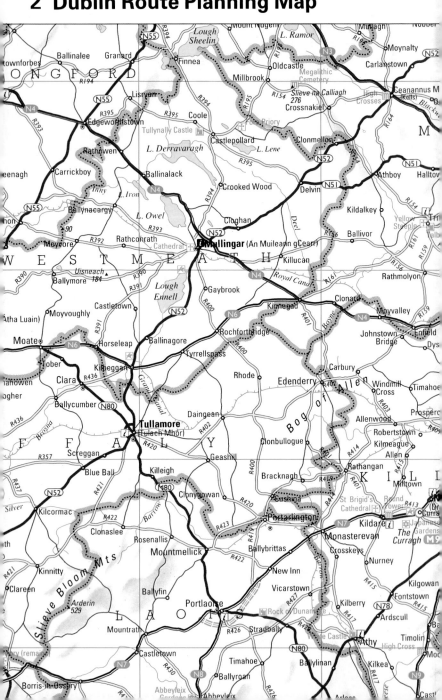

IRISH SEA

Woodtown
Clogher Hd
246 ▲ Collon
R168
Clogherhead
Monasterboice
Termonfeckin
Mellifont Abbey
Tullyallen
R167
Baltray
Vilkinstown
N2
Hill of Slane
Drogheda (Droichead Átha)
R163
Slane
N31
Boyne
R150
R151
Kilberry Knowthcomb
Dowth Tomb
Bettystown
Newgrange
Newgrange Tomb
R108
Julianstown
Knowmore Round
Tower and Church
R150
R152
R150
Navan
(An Uaimh)
R153
Duleek
Gormanston
Garlowcross
R152
Ardcath
Stamullen
Balbriggan
Abbey
Balrath
Four Knocks
Megalithic Tomb
Hill of Tara
154 ▲
Garristown
R130
Naul
R172
Skerries
R108
R128
Dunshaughlin
R125
Oldtown
Ashbourne
R122
Ballyboghil
Lusk
Rush
R125
Ratoath
R129
Fairyhouse
R126
Portrane
Lambay I.
merhill
N3
R154
Kilbride
R125
Donabate
R156
Swords
N1
Malahide
R106
Dunboyne
DUBLIN
Portmarnock
Clonee
Dunsoghly Castle
M1
Coolock
Ireland's Eye
Maynooth
M4
Blanchardstown
Botanic
Howth
N4
Leixlip
Power Station
Drumcondra
R105
Clontarf
Castletown House
Lucan
Palmerston
Dublin Bay
Celbridge
Grand Canal
M50
Terenure
DUBLIN (BAILE ÁTHA CLIATH)
Straffan
R403
Liffey
Clondalkin
N1
Clane
Newcastle
TALLAGHT
Rathfarnham
DÚN LAOGHAIRE
Rathcoole
Saggart
R114
James Joyce Tower
Kill
N81
Dundrum
Stillorgan
Dalkey
Saltins
Brittas
R114
R113
R119
Ballybrack
M7
Naas (An Nás)
Kilteel
R115
R116
Loughlinstown
Kilbride
Glencullen
R117
Blessington
Kippure
▲ 754
Enniskerry
Bray (Bré)
Russborough Ho
Pollaphuca
Lakes
Djouce Mt
886 ▲
Gt Sugar Loaf
506 ▲
Kilmacanogue
R761
Ballymore
Eustace
Greystones
Valleymount
Mullaghcleevaun
▲ 850
Varty
Res
Delgany
Hollywood
Ballynockan
R765
Kilcoole
Newtownmountkennedy
Tonelagee
▲ 819
Roundwood
R764
Newcastle
N81
Ashford
Mt Usher Gardens
Donard
Glendalough
Laragh
Avonmore
Ashford
664 ▲
Glenealy
Rathnew
N11
Wicklow (Cill Mhantáin)
Knockanarrigan
926 ▲
Lugnaquilla
Mt
R752
Wicklow Head
Baltinglass
Rathdrum
Kilbride
Ardmore Pt
Rathdangan
Aghavannagh
Avondale
Forest Park

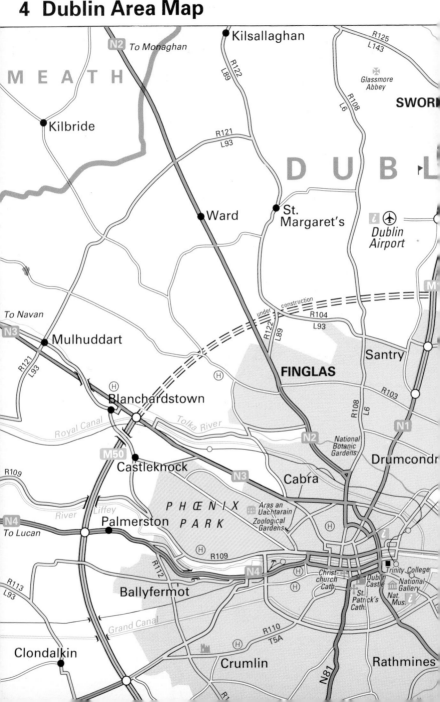

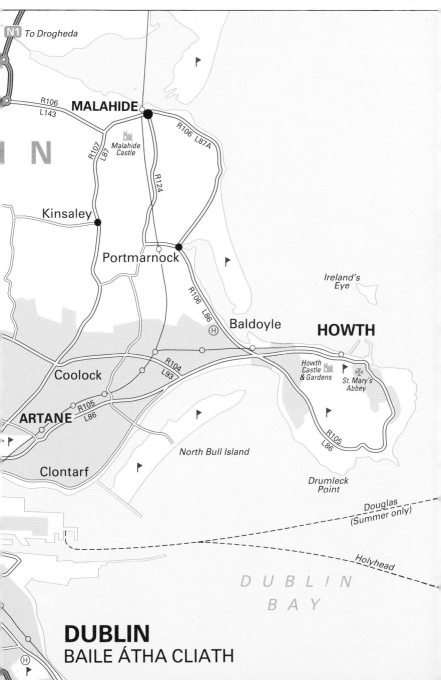

N1 To Drogheda

R106
L143
MALAHIDE

R106 L87A

R107
L87

Malahide
Castle

R124

Kinsaley

Portmarnock

R106 L86

Baldoyle

HOWTH

Ireland's
Eye

Howth
Castle
& Gardens

St. Mary's
Abbey

Coolock

R104
L93

R105
L86

ARTANE

North Bull Island

Clontarf

R105
L86

Drumleck
Point

Douglas
(Summer only)

Holyhead

D U B L I N

B A Y

DUBLIN
BAILE ÁTHA CLIATH

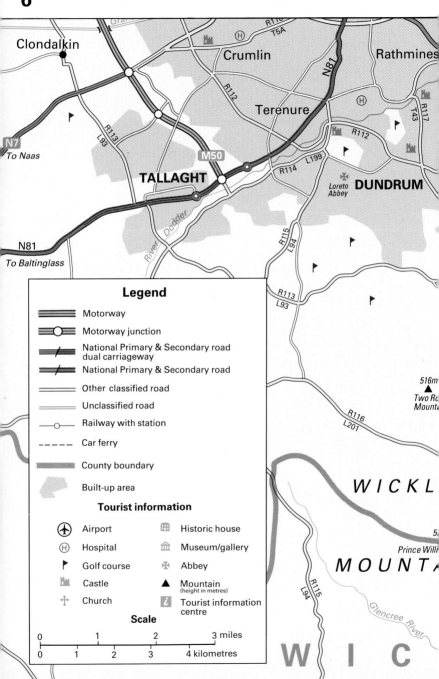

Clondalkin

Crumlin

Rathmines

R116
T5A

N7
To Naas

R112

Terenure

R113

L93

R112

T43

M50

TALLAGHT

R114

L199

DUNDRUM

Loreto
Abbey

N81
To Baltinglass

River Dodder

R115

L94

R113

L93

516m
Two Ro
Mount

R116
L201

WICKL

Prince Willi

MOUNTA

L201

R115

L94

Glencree River

WIC

Legend

	Motorway
	Motorway junction
	National Primary & Secondary road dual carriageway
	National Primary & Secondary road
	Other classified road
	Unclassified road
	Railway with station
	Car ferry
	County boundary
	Built-up area

Tourist information

✈	Airport	⊞	Historic house
Ⓗ	Hospital	🏛	Museum/gallery
▶	Golf course	✠	Abbey
🏰	Castle	▲	Mountain (height in metres)
✝	Church	𝒊	Tourist information centre

Scale

0   1   2   3 miles
0   1   2   3   4 kilometres

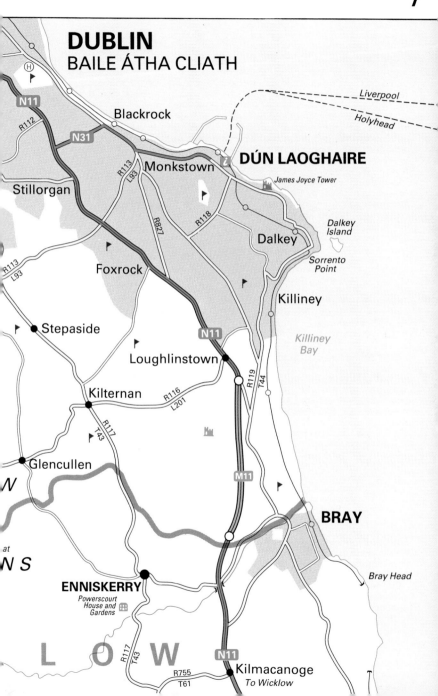

DUBLIN
BAILE ÁTHA CLIATH

Liverpool

Holyhead

N11

R112

N31

Blackrock

DÚN LAOGHAIRE

Monkstown

James Joyce Tower

R113

L93

Stillorgan

R118

R827

Dalkey Island

Dalkey

Sorrento Point

Foxrock

R113

L93

Killiney

Killiney Bay

Stepaside

N11

Loughlinstown

R119

T44

Kilternan

R116

L201

R117

T43

Glencullen

N

M11

BRAY

Bray Head

ENNISKERRY
Powerscourt House and Gardens

at

N S

L O W

R117

T43

N11

R755

T61

Kilmacanoge
To Wicklow

8 Dublin City Guide

HISTORY

The ford over the River Liffey has been important since Celtic times, and there was a thriving Christian community here from the 5thC, following their conversion by St Patrick in AD448. In AD840 the marauding Vikings landed here, built a fortress on the high ground and established a settlement along the banks of the estuary. Originally a base for their numerous raiding sorties, it soon became a flourishing trading port as well, but Viking dominance was severely curtailed following a defeat by Brian Boru at the Battle of Clontarf in 1014.

Converted by Christianity, the Vikings were finally driven out by the Anglo-Normans under Strongbow, who took Dublin by storm, executing the Viking leader, Hasculf. In 1172 Henry II, having established his feudal rights over the invading force, received the submission of the Irish chieftains on the site of College Green. He granted the city by charter to the men of Bristol, from whence the Anglo-Normans had originally come.

The city and surrounding area, established as the seat of English government and protected by an enclosing wall and strategic castles, was known as The Pale. Frequently attacked during the 12thC and 13thC by the Irish clans based in the Wicklow Mountains, it was assaulted unsuccessfully by Edward Bruce in 1316. The city witnessed the crowning of Lambert Simnel, pretender to the English throne, in Christ Church in 1486. Unmoved by the rebellion of 'Silken' Thomas Fitzgerald in 1534, the inhabitants remained loyal to the English crown, supporting King Charles during the Civil Wars. Captured by the Parliamentarians in 1647, the city underwent a great architectural expansion following the Restoration of Charles II. During the Williamite wars Dublin was a Jacobite stronghold. It was here that James II held his last parliament in 1689.

By the end of the 17thC, Dublin was already a flourishing commercial centre; public street lighting had been introduced in 1697 and during the following century the city was transformed into one of the handsomest of Georgian cities. The 'Wide Streets Commission' was established in 1757 and in 1773 the Paving Board was formed. New, elegantly spacious streets and squares were planned and palatial town houses built. In 1783 the Irish Parliament was granted a short-lived autonomy but there was growing political unrest, which erupted in the uprising of 1798. Lord Edward Fitzgerald died of wounds sustained resisting arrest and in 1800 the detested Act of Union was established and the fortunes of the city began to wane.

With government now in London, few of the noblemen required their fine mansions and many returned to their country estates or left for London. Bitterness increased; in 1803 the Lord Chief Justice was assassinated and Robert Emmet, the leader of an abortive insurrection, was hanged. The newspaper *The Nation* was established by Charles Gavan Duffy in 1842, the heyday of the Repeal Movement. In 1841 Daniel O'Connell was elected Lord Mayor; only three years later he was interned in Richmond Gaol for campaigning for the repeal of the Union and the restoration of Grattan's 'Irish Parliament'. In 1873 the first great Home Rule Conference was held. In 1879 the Land League was formed, whose leaders, including Parnell and Davitt, were imprisoned for their pains. In 1882 the new Chief Secretary, Lord Frederick Cavendish, and his Under-Secretary were assassinated in Phoenix Park by the Invincibles, a new terrorist organisation. As the campaign for Home Rule gathered momentum, the Gaelic League, which started the Irish literary renaissance, was established by Douglas Hyde and Eóin MacNeill in 1893. Conceived as a means of reviving interest in the Irish language and traditional Irish life, the Gaelic League was also responsible for a remarkable literary revival resulting in the formation of the Abbey Theatre in 1904, where plays by J M Synge, Sean O'Casey and W B Yeats, amongst others, were performed.

In 1905 the Sinn Fein movement was formed, in 1909 the Irish Transport and General Workers Union was set up under the leadership of James Connolly, and in 1913 there was a massive strike, paralysing the city. In 1914 the Irish Volunteers came into being, largely to combat the Ulster Volunteers. These latter were raised by Edward Carson in January 1913 to defend the right of Ulster to remain united with Great Britain. In 1916 the Irish Volunteers seized the Post Office in Lower O'Connell Street as their headquarters and the Easter Rising had begun. It was quickly crushed, but so brutally that public conscience, clearly appalled, overwhelmingly elected Sinn Fein at the general election of December 1918 with de Valera as the new president. Whilst the Dublin faction was openly in support of the guerrilla bands operating across the country, the Ulster Unionists set up their own provisional government, and the ambushes and assassinations which characterised the Anglo-Irish War, featuring the notorious Black and Tans, began in bloody earnest. The war ended in the truce of July 1921. Despite the ratification of the Irish Free State in January 1922, a large and dissatisfied faction of leaders in the Irish movement took up arms against their former comrades and seized the Four Courts, which they held for two months. The subsequent shelling ordered by the new Dublin Government destroyed much of O'Connell Street but by the 1930s most of the public buildings had been restored.

TOURIST INFORMATION OFFICES

Suffolk Street	(01) 605 7799
Dun Laoghaire Ferry Terminal	
	(01) 284 6361
Arrivals Hall, Dublin Airport	
	(01) 844 5997
Baggott Street Bridge	(01) 602 4229
Tallaght	(01) 462 0671

TOURIST TELEPHONE SERVICES

Local/National Credit Card Reservation (Accomodation)	(01) 605 7777
Telephone	(01) 605 7799
Fax	(01) 605 7707

VISITOR INFORMATION SERVICE

(24hr) (Premium Rate)	
Ireland only	1550 112233
Overseas	(01) 605 7797

CATHEDRALS AND CHURCHES

Augustinian Church Thomas Street.
Designed by E W Pugin and G C Ashlin in 1862 it has a mountainous exterior with lofty side aisles to the nave and 160 foot high tower crowned by a spire.
Christ Church Cathedral Christchurch Place.
The Cathedral was founded by Strongbow in 1173 on the site of a church founded in 1038 by Dunan, Bishop of Dublin. It is, along with St. Patrick's, one of the best examples in Ireland of early Gothic architecture and was extensively restored btween 1871-78 by George Edmund Street.
Franciscan Church Merchant's Quay.
Designed by Patrick Byrne in 1830.
St Anne's Church Dawson Street.
Designed by Isaac Wells in 1720 with a Romanesque-style facade added by Sir Thomas Deane in 1868.
St Audoen's Church High Street.
Dublin's only surviving medieval church, with a portal of 1190. The bell tower, restored in the 19thC, has three 15thC bells.
St Audoen's RC Church High Street.
Designed by Patrick Byrne in 1841-47, it has a monumental, cliff-like exterior with a huge Corinthian portico added by Stephen Ashlin in 1898.
St George's Temple Street.
This neo-classical church was designed by Francis Johnston in 1802 and has a 200 foot high steeple modelled on St Martin-in-the Fields, London.
St Mary's Mary Street.
A handsome galleried church designed by Thomas Burgh in 1627.
St Mary's Abbey Meetinghouse Lane.
A Cistercian foundation, established in 1139, whose remains include a fine vaulted Chapter House of 1190.
St Mary's Pro-Cathedral Cathedral Street.
A Greek Doric style building, built 1815-25 by John Sweetman and modelled on the Church of St Philippe, rue St Honore, Paris.
St Michan's Church Church Street.
Founded in 1095 and largely rebuilt in 1685. Famous for the mummified bodies in the crypt and its fine 18thC organ.
St Patrick's Cathedral Patrick Street.
The National Cathedral of the Church of Ireland, it was built between 1220-54 and was restored in the 19thC.
St Saviour's Dominick Street.
Designed by J J McCarthy in 1858 this extravagant French style Gothic edifice has a bold west door under a triangular hood, crowned by a large rose window.
St Stephen's Mount Street Crescent.
Designed by John Bowden in 1824 this handsome neo-classical church has a Erechtheon inspired Greek style portico.

St Werburgh's Church Werburgh Street. Originally the site of an Anglo-Norman foundation, the present church was built in 1715-19 and rebuilt in 1759-68, following a fire.

Whitefriar Street Carmelite Church Stands on the site of a pre-Reformation Carmelite Priory.

INTERESTING BUILDINGS

Bank of Ireland College Green. Designed by Sir Edward Lovett Pearce in 1729. It was originally the Parliament House; the first of a series of great public buildings erected in 18thC Dublin.

City Hall Lord Edward Street. Completed in 1779, this fine building was designed as The Royal Exchange. It features a beautiful coffered dome.

Custom House Custom House Quay. This masterpiece was designed by James Gandon in 1781 and although not open to the public, has a magnificent long river frontage.

Dublin Castle Cork Hill, Dame Street. The Castle was originally built 1204-28 as part of Dublin's defensive system. The Record or Wardrobe Tower is the principal remnant of the 13thC Anglo-Norman fortress and has walls 16 foot thick.

The 15thC Bermingham Tower was once the state prison where Red Hugh O'Donnell was interned in the 16thC. Of interest are the State Apartments, dating from the British Administration; these were once the residence of English Viceroys.

Four Courts Inns Quay. Originally designed by James Gandon in 1785, it was destroyed by a fire in 1922 but later rebuilt. Four Courts has a 450 foot river frontage and a square central block with circular hall, crowned by a shallow dome carried in a high columned drum.

General Post Office O'Connell Street. Designed by Francis Johnston and completed in 1818. The 1916 Easter Rising started here.

Guinness Brewery Crane Street. Established in 1759 and is now the largest exporting brewery in the world. The Guinness Hop Store is open to the public Mon - Fri 10 a m to 3 p m. Tel: 4536700.

Kilmainham Jail Inchicore. Built in 1796. Countless patriots have been imprisoned here including Emmet and his United Irishmen colleagues, the Fenians, the Invincibles and the Irish Volunteers of the Easter Rising. It was closed in 1924 and re-opened as a museum in 1966.

King's Inns Constitution Hill and Henrietta Street. A glorious classical edifice, partly built to the plans of James Gandon. The courtyard joins Henrietta Street where one can see Dublin's earliest Georgian mansions.

Leinster House Kildare Street. Originally a handsome town mansion designed by Richard Castle for the Earl of Kildare in 1745; it has been the Parliament House since 1922.

Malahide Castle Malahide. Originally built in 1185, it was the seat of the Talbot family from 1185-1976. Now in public ownership, it displays a large part of the National Portrait collection and the Fry Model Railway Museum.

Marino Casino Malahide Road. A miniature Palladian style masterpiece designed by Sir William Chambers in 1762. Built as a little pleasure house beside Lord Charlemont's country residence for the enormous sum of £60,000, it's a remarkably compact building planned in a Greek cross articulated by both free standing columns and pilasters with rusticated main walls. The circular hall inside, ringed by columns, is crowned by a coffered dome. The graceful urns crowning the attic storey are chimneys.

Mansion House Dawson Street. Built in 1705, it has been the official residence of the Lord Mayor of Dublin since 1715.

Newman House St Stephen's Green. Built in 1765 for Richard Whaley MP with plasterwork by Robert West, the house has also been owned by the celebrated gambler Buck Whaley.

Number 29 Lower Fitzwilliam Street. This typical four-storey-over-basement street house has been restored and furnished exactly as it would have been during the late 18thC.

Powerscourt House South William Street. A classical style mansion designed by Robert Mack and built between 1771-74, now a lively centre of shops, cafés and restaurants.

Royal Hospital Kilmainham

Dublin's only monumental 17thC building was built as a home for army pensioners and has one of Dublin's finest interiors. It also houses the Irish Museum of Modern Art.

Trinity College College Green.
The original Elizabethan college was founded in 1592 but the present building was built between 1755-1759. The cruciform complex wrapped around quadrangles and gardens has an impressive 300 foot Palladian facade designed by Henry Keene and John Sanderford.

The library's great treasures include the 8thC Book of Kells, the Book of Durrow, the Book of Armagh and the Liber Hymnorum.

PLACES OF INTEREST

Arbour Hill Collins Barracks.
Cemetery where the leaders of the Easter Rising are buried.

Ashtown Castle Visitor Centre Pheonix Park.
The oldest building in the park has now been renovated and houses a visitor centre.

Drimnagh Castle Long Mile Road.
Ireland's only castle with a flooded moat. This 13thC castle now has a fully restored Great Hall and 17thC style garden which is open to the public.

Dublin Experience, The Trinity College.
An audiovisual presentation of the story of Dublin.

Dunsink Observatory between Finglas and Blanchardstown.
Founded in 1783, it is one of the oldest observatories in the world. Public nights are held on the first and third Saturdays of each month from September to March inclusive at 8 p m - 10 p m.

Garden of Remembrance Parnell Square.
The Garden of Remembrance, opened in 1966, dedicated to all those who died in the cause of Irish Freedom.

Ha'penny Bridge Crampton Quay.
An elegant pedestrian bridge spanning the Liffey.

Irish Whiskey Corner Bow Street.
Old warehouse converted into exhibition centre.

Temple Bar This charming area is Dublin's Bohemian quarter. With its narrow cobbled streets running close to the Liffey it is full of character. It is home to artists and musicians of all styles and talents.

Wood Quay by Christchurch Cathedral.
Modern office blocks and new civic offices occupy this site which was once the 9th - 11thC Viking city of Dublin.

MUSEUMS

Dublin Civic Museum South William Street. Tel: 6794260.
Permanent exhibition about the city of Dublin.

Dublin Writers Museum Parnell Square North. Tel: 8722077.
Traces the history of Irish literature from its earliest times to the 20thC.

Dublinia Christ Church Tel: 6794611
A realistic sight-and-sound recreation of Dublin in medieval times.

Guinness Hop Store Crane Street.
Tel: 4536700. Mon-Fri 10am - 4.30pm
Documentary films and exhibition about the company's development.

Heraldic Museum Kildare Street Tel: 6618811
Illustrates the uses of heraldry and is the only one of its kind in the world.

Irish Architectural Archive Merrion Square. Tel: 6763430.

Irish-Jewish Museum 3 Walworth Road. Tel: 4531797

Irish Museum of Modern Art Royal Hospital, Kilmainham. Tel: 6718666.

James Joyce Cultural Centre North Great George's Street Tel: 8731984.
A museum in a Georgian mansion, built in 1784, devoted to the great novelist.

James Joyce Museum Sandycove. Tel: 2809265.
Personal possessions, photographs, first editions and items about James Joyce.

Kilmainham Jail Inchicore Road. Tel: 4535984.
Museum dedicated to the Irish patriots imprisoned there from 1792-1924.

Museum of Childhood Palmerston Park, Rathmines. Tel: 4973223.
Charming private collection of antique dolls and toys.

National Maritime Museum Haigh Terrace, Dun Laoghaire. Tel: 2800969.
Traces the history of Irish Literature from its earliest times up to the 20thC.

National Museum Kildare Street. Tel: 6618811
Houses a fabulous collection of national

antiquities including Bronze Age gold ornaments.

National Wax Museum Granby Row.
Tel: 8726340.
Wax replicas of well-known persons and scenes.

Natural History Museum Merrion Street.
Tel: 6618811
Houses a collection of preserved animals and the remains of extinct mammals and birds.

Number 29 Lower Fitzwilliam Street
Tel: 7026165
A completely restored middle class house of the late 18thC.

Shaw Birthplace, The Synge Street
Tel: 4750854
The birthplace of one of Ireland's three Nobel prizewinners for literature.

Waterways Visitor Centre Grand Canal Basin, Ringsend Tel: 6777510/6613111.
A centre built on piers over the canal, housing an exhibition of Ireland's waterways.

LIBRARIES

Central Library Ilac Centre. Tel: 8734333.
Central Catholic Library Merrion Square.
Tel: 6761264.
Religious and general interest, with a large Irish section.

Chester Beatty Library & Gallery of Oriental Art Shrewsbury Road.
Tel: 2692386. Tue-Fri 10-5pm, Sat 2-5pm
Houses one of the finest collections of oriental manuscripts and miniatures in the world.

Goethe Institute Library Merrion Square.
Tel: 6611155.
A business information centre.

Kings Inns Henrietta Street. Tel: 8744840.
Founded 1787, contains over 100,000 books and copies of almost all of the Dublin directories ever published.

Marsh's Library St Patrick's Close.
Tel: 6753917. 4543511.
Opened in 1701, contains many rare books.

National Library Kildare Street.
Tel: 6618811
Offers over half a million books, as well as a vast collection of maps, prints and manuscripts and an invaluable collection of Irish newspapers.

Pearse Street Library Pearse Street.
Tel: 6777662.
Irish interest books including references

to local printing and bookbinding.

Royal Irish Academy 19 Dawson Street.
Tel: 6762570, 6764222.
One of the largest collections of ancient Irish manuscripts in the country.

Trinity College Library College Green.
Tel: 7022320.
The oldest and most famous of Dublin's libraries; it houses over a million books plus a magnificent collection of early illuminated manuscripts, including the famous Book of Kells.

Other general and reference libraries:
Dublin Diocesan Library Clonliffe Road.
Tel: 8741680.
Genealogical Office Kildare Street.
Tel: 6618811.
Gilbert Library Pearse Street.
Tel: 6777662.

GALLERIES, ARTS CENTRES, CONCERT AND EXHIBITION HALLS

City Arts Centre Moss Street
Tel: 6770643
A new complex of galleries, exhibition areas and theatre space for local groups and artists.

Davis Gallery Capel Street. Tel: 8726969.
Douglas Hyde Gallery Trinity College.
Tel: 7021116.
Gallery of Photography Wellington Quay. Tel: 6714654.
Hugh Lane Municipal Gallery of Modern Art Parnell Square, Hugh Lane.
Tel: 8741903.
National Concert Hall Earlsfort Terrace.
Tel: 6711888.
National Gallery Merrion Square West.
Tel: 6615133.
Neptune Gallery South William Street.
Tel: 6715021.
Oliver Dowling Kildare Street.
Tel: 6766573.
Oriel Gallery Clare Street. Tel: 6763410.
Project Arts Centre East Essex.
Tel: 6712321.
Royal Dublin Society Ballsbridge.
Tel: 6680645, 6680866.
Solomon Gallery Powerscourt Centre.
Tel: 6794237.
Taylor Galleries Kildare St.
Tel: 6766055.
Tom Caldwell Gallery Fitzwilliam Street Upper. Tel: 6688629
United Arts Club Fitzwilliam Street Upper. Tel: 6762965.

PARKS AND GARDENS
Marley Park
Situated in Rathfarnham this large park contains areas of woodland, a large pond, nature trail and model railway.
National Botanic Gardens
Located in Glesnevin, it provides 50 acres of magnificent gardens with a fabulous collection of plants, shrubs and trees; established in 1790. Many of the plants come from tropical Africa and South America.
Phoenix Park
Phoenix Park, covering over 1,760 acres, is the best-known park in Ireland. Enclosed by an 8 mile long stone wall, the park was laid out in the mid 18thC and was the scene of the Phoenix Park murders in 1882, when the Chief Secretary and Under-Secretary for Ireland were assassinated. The park includes a number of buildings, the most important of which is Aras an Uachtarain; a private house built in 1751, it later became the house of the President of Ireland when Dr Douglas Hyde moved there in 1938. Other buildings are the houses of the Pope's ambassador and the American ambassador; St Mary's Hospital with handsome chapel by Thomas Cooley of 1771; the Magazine Fort of 1734. There is the people's gardens by the main entrance on Parkgate Street, and a zoo.
St Anne's Park
St Anne's Park, to the north east in Dollymount, is a large park covering over 270 acres and wooded with evergreen, oak, pine, beech, chestnut and lime. There is a lovely rose garden, opened in 1975. Formerly the house of the Guinness Family.
St Stephen's Green
In the heart of the city, St Stephen's Green was originally an open common, enclosed in 1663. The earliest as well as the largest of Dublin's squares, it is encircled by magnificent 18thC and 19thC buildings, in particular No 85, by Richard Castle in 1739; No 86 by Robert West in 1765; on the west side, Nos 119-20 by Richard Castle and the Royal College of Surgeons by Edward Pike in 1806. The Green itself was opened to the general public in 1877.
Zoological Gardens
The Zoological Gardens, inside Phoenix Park, are famous for the breeding of lions and other 'big cats'. The zoo has attractive gardens encircling two natural lakes where pelicans, flamingoes, ducks and geese abound.

ENTERTAINMENT, FOOD AND DRINK
CABARET
Abbey Tavern Howth. Tel: 8390282.
Braemor Rooms Churchtown. Tel: 2988664.
Burlington Hotel Leeson Street Upper. Tel: 6605222.
Clontarf Castle Clontarf. Tel: 8332321.
Jury's Hotel Ballsbridge. Tel: 6605000.

RESTAURANTS
Ante Room Baggot Street Lower. Tel: 6604716
Grey Door, The Pembroke Street Upper. Tel: 6763286.
Guinea Pig Dalkey. Tel: 2859055.
King Sitric Howth. Tel: 8325235.
Le Coq Hardi Ballsbridge. Tel: 6689070.
Lord Edward Christchurch. Tel: 4542420.
Old Dublin Francis Street. Tel: 4542028.
Restaurant Na Mara Dun Laoghaire. Tel: 2806767.
Rolys Bistro Ballsbridge. Tel: 6682611

PUBS AND CLUBS
Abbey Tavern (trad music) Howth. Tel: 8390307.
Bailey, The Duke Street. Tel: 6773055.
Black Lion Inn Emmet Road. Inchicore. Tel: 4534580.
Bowes Fleet Street. Tel: 6714038.
Brazen Head Bridge Street Lower. Tel: 6795186.
Cross Guns Phibsboro. Tel: 8301216
Davy Byrnes Duke Street. Tel: 6711298.
Doheny and Nesbitts Lower Baggot Street. Tel: 6760655.
Hourican Leeson Street. Tel: 6762634.
Humphreys Ranelagh. Tel: 4972490.
Kitty O'Shea's Grand Canal Street. Tel: 6609965.
Long Hall Great George Street. Tel: 4751590.
McDaids Harry Street. Tel: 6794395.
Mulligans Poolbeg Street. Tel: 6775582.
O'Donoghues (trad music) Merrion Row. Tel: 6614303.
Orchard Inn Killincarrig Delgany. Tel: 2874631.

Palace Bar Fleet Street. Tel: 6779290.
Ryans Parkgate Street. Tel: 6776097.
Slattery's (trad music) Rathmines Road.
Tel: 4972052.
Stag's Head Dame Court. Tel: 6793701.
Tamango Sands Hotel (night club)
Portmarnock. Tel: 8460003.

THEATRES
Abbey Theatre Abbey Street Lower 1.
Tel: 8787222.
Andrews Lane Theatre Tel: 6795720.
Focus Theatre Pembroke Place,
Pembroke Street 2. Tel: 6763071.
Gaiety Theatre South King Street 2.
Tel: 6771717.
Gate Theatre Cavendish Row, Parnell
Square. Tel: 8744045.
Lambert Puppet Theatre Clifton Lane,
Monkstown. Tel: 2800974.
Olympia Theatre 74 Dame Street 2.
Tel: 6777744.
Peacock Theatre Abbey Street Lower 1.
Tel: 8787222.
Project Arts Centre 39 East Essex Street.
Tel: 6712321.
Tivoli Theatre Francis Street.
Tel: 4544472.

CINEMAS
Adelphia Cinema Mid Abbey Street.
Tel: 8730433.
Classic Cinema Harold's Cross Road 6.
Tel: 4923324
Forum Cinema Dun Laoghaire.
Tel: 2809574.
Irish Film Centre Eustace Street.
Tel: 6778788
Lighthouse Cinema Middle Abbey
Street. Tel: 8730438.
M.G.M. Multiplex Parnell Street (July
1995)
Omniplex 10 Screen Santry. Tel: 8428844
Ormonde Cinema Stillorgan Plaza,
Stillorgan. Tel; 2831144.
Savoy Cinema 19 O'Connell Street
Upper 1. Tel: 8746000.
Screen at College Street Tel: 6714988
Stella Picture Theatre Ltd 207 Rathmines
Road Lower 6. Tel: 4971281.
UCI Coolock Tel: 8485133.
UCI Tallaght Tel: 4522611.

PASSENGER TRAVEL
CAR FERRIES
Passenger and vehicle ferry services are:
Brittany Ferries Tourist House, 42 Grand
Parade, Cork. Tel: Cork 277801.
Services: Cork-Roscoff, Cork-Swansea.
Irish Ferries 16 Westmoreland Street,
Dublin 2. Tel: 6610511.
Services: Dublin-Holyhead, Rosslare-
Pembroke.
Irish Ferries Merrion Row, Dublin 2.
Tel: 6610511.
Services: Rosslare-Le Havre, Rosslare-
Cherbourg.
Stena Sealink Haddington Terrace, Dun
Laoghaire. Tel: 2807777
Services: Dun Laoghaire-Holyhead,
Rosslare-Fishguard, Larne-Stranraer.

RAIL & BUS TRAVEL
Dublin is linked with the cities and towns
of Ireland by a network of rail and bus
services operated by Coras Iompair
Eireann (CIE), which is Ireland's National
Internal Transport Authority.

All information regarding rail and road
services can be obtained from: CIE, 59
O'Connell Street Upper, Dublin 1.
Tel: 8720000.

HOTELS
Ashling Parkgate Street. Tel: 6772324.
Avalon House Aungier Street.
Tel: 4750001.
Berkeley Court Lansdowne Road.
Tel: 6601711.
Burlington Leeson Street. Tel: 6605222.
Buswells Molesworth Street.
Tel: 6764013.
Fitzpatricks Castle Killiney. Tel: 2840700.
Forte Crest Dublin Airport.
Tel: 8379211.
Green Isle Naas Road, Clondalkin.
Tel: 4593406.
Gresham O'Connell Street Upper.
Tel: 8746881.
Jury's Ballsbridge. Tel: 6605000.
Jury's Christchurch. Tel: 4750111
Kildare Hotel & Country Club Straffan.
Tel: 6273333
Montrose Stillorgan Road. Tel: 2693311.
Mount Herbert Herbert Road.
Tel: 6684321.
Royal Dublin O'Connell Street.
Tel: 8733666.

Royal Marine Hotel Dun Laoghaire.
Tel: 2801911.
Sands Strand Road, Portmarnock.
Tel: 8460003.
Shelbourne St Stephen's Green.
Tel: 6766471.
Skylon Upper Drumcondra Road.
Tel: 8379121.
Spa Lucan. Tel: 6280494.
Tara Towers Merrion Road. Tel: 2694666.
Westbury Clarendon Street.
Tel: 6791122.

SHOPPING
Arnott's Henry Street. Tel: 8721111.
Brown Thomas Grafton Street.
Tel: 6776821.
Clery and Co O'Connell Street.
Tel: 8786000.
Janelle Shopping Centre Fingles.
Tel: 8361227.
Marks & Spencers Grafton Street.
Tel: 6797855.
Penney's Stores Mary Street.
Tel: 8727788.
Roches Stores Henry Street. Tel: 8730044.

SUPERMARKET CHAINS
There are several branches of each of the following supermarkets in Dublin: Quinnsworth, Superquinn, Crazy Prices and Dunnes Stores.

BOOKSHOPS
Alan Hanna Bookshop Rathmines.
Tel: 4967398.
Book Shop Rathfarnham Shopping Centre. Tel: 4934733.
Book Stop Blackrock Shopping Centre.
Tel: 2832193.
Book Stop Dun Laoghaire Shopping Centre. Tel: 2809917.
Books Upstairs College Green.
Tel: 6796687.
Books Upstairs Omni. Tel: 8421210
Bray Bookshop Bray. Tel: 2869370.
Dublin Bookshop Grafton Street.
Tel: 6775568.
Dubray Swan Centre Rathmines.
Tel: 4979722
Eason The Square. Tallaght. Tel: 4524855.
Eason & Son Ltd O'Connell Street Lower.
Tel: 8733811.
Eason Dun Laoghaire Georges Street.
Tel: 2805528.

Eason Ilac Centre Mary Street.
Tel: 8721322.
Eason Irish Life Centre Talbot Street.
Tel: 8727010.
Eblana Bookshop Slaney Drive.
Tel: 8301111.
Fred Hanna Ltd Nassau Street.
Tel: 6771255.
Geo. Webb Crampton Quay.
Tel: 6777489.
Greene & Co Clare Street. Tel: 6762554.
Hodges Figgis Dawson Street.
Tel: 6774754.
Hughes and Hughes St Stephens Green.
Tel: 4783060.
Hughes and Hughes Nutgrove.
Tel: 4932957.
Hughes and Hughes Airport. Tel: 837990
Paperback Centre Stillorgan Shopping Centre. Tel: 2886341.
Waterstone's Dawson Street.
Tel: 6791415.
Wicklow St. Bookshop. Tel: 6688328

BOOK WHOLESALERS
Argosy Libraries 3 Portside Business Centre, Eastwall Road, Dublin 3
Tel: 8552727
Eason Wholesale Brickfield Drive, Crumlin. Tel: 4536211
Hughes & Hughes 21 Lee Road, Dublin Industrial Estate. Tel: 8304811

MARKETS
Iveagh Market (old clothes, furniture etc.) Francis Street.
Liberty Market (clothes, fabrics, household goods) Meath Street.
Moore Street Market (fruit and vegetables) off Henry Street.
Mother Redcaps Fri-Sun only Christchurch Back Lane. Tel: 4544655
Vegetable Market (fruit, vegetables, fish and flowers) St Mitchan's Street.

SPORTS VENUES
Athletics (International Venue)
Croke Park GAA - Tel: 8363222.

Bathing, Beaches
There are safe sandy beaches at:
Ballyfermot - Le Fanu Park
Ballymun - Seven Towers Shopping Centre.
Claremount - 9 miles from Dublin.

Coolock - Northside Shopping Centre.
Crumlin - Windmill Road.
Dollymount - 3½ miles from Dublin.
Donabate - 13 miles from Dublin.
Finglas - Mellowes Road.
Iveagh Baths - Bride Street.
Malahide - 9 miles from Dublin.
Portmarnock - 9 miles from Dublin.
Rathmines - Williams Park.
Sean McDermott Street - City Centre.
Sutton - 7 miles from Dublin.
There are outdoor swimming baths, open from June to September, at: *Blackrock, Clontarf, Dun Laoghaire.*

Bowling Centres
Dundrum Bowl - Sandyford Road, Dundrum 14. Tel: 2980209.
Stillorgan Bowl - Stillorgan. Tel: 2881656.
Tallagh Sportsbowl. Tel: 4599411

Flying
Weston Aerodrome - Celbridge Road, Lucan. Tel: 6280435.

Football (International Venue)
Dalymount Park

Golf
18-hole golf clubs:
Beaverstown Golf Club - 10 miles from Dublin.
Beech Park - 10 miles from Dublin.
Castle Golf Club - Rathfarnham, 4 miles from Dublin.
Castlewarden Golf Club - 12 miles from Dublin
Clontarf Golf Club - 2½ miles from Dublin.
Donabate - 13 miles from Dublin.
Dun Laoghaire - 7 miles from Dublin.
Edmondstown - 6 miles from Dublin.
Elm Park - 3½ miles from Dublin.
Forrest Little Golf Club - 5½ miles from Dublin.
Grange Rathfarnham - 6 miles from Dublin.
Hermitage Lucan - 7¼ miles from Dublin.
Howth - 9 miles from Dublin.
Island Malahide - 9 miles from Dublin.
Lucan - 8 miles from Dublin.
Luttrelstown Golf & Country Club - 6 miles from Dublin
Milltown - 4½ miles from Dublin.
Newlands Clondalkin - 6 miles from Dublin.
Portmarnock - 9 miles from Dublin.
Royal Dublin - Dollymount, 3 miles from Dublin.

St. Margarets Golf Club - 8 miles from Dublin.
Slade Valley - Saggart, 9 miles from Dublin.
Stackstown - 9 miles from Dublin.
Westmanstown - 6 miles from Dublin.
Woodbrook - near Bray, 11½ miles from Dublin.

Greyhound Racing
Greyhound racing is one of Ireland's leading spectator sports. Meetings are held at:
Shelbourne Park Stadium - Ringsend (Mon, Wed and Sat at 8 pm).
Harold's Cross Stadium - (Tues, Thur and Fri at 8 pm).

Horse Racing
There are two racecourses on the outskirts of Dublin:
Leopardstown - 6 miles from Dublin.
Fairyhouse - 12 miles from Dublin.

Ice Skating
Dublin Ice Rink - Dolphins Barn. Tel: 4534153.

Leisure Centre (various sports)
Ballyfermot

Rugby (International Venue)
Lansdowne Road - Tel: 6689300.

Sports Clubs
Amateur Football League - Tel: 8483777.
Badminton Hall - Tel: 4505966.
Ballyboden/St Edna's GAA - Tel: 4947950.
Blackrock RFC - Tel: 2805967.
Castleknock Lawn Tennis Club - Tel: 8210423.
Clontarf Cricket and Football Club - Tel: 8336214.
Clontarf Yacht and Boat Club - Tel: 8332691.
Craobh Chiarain GAA - Tel: 8311050.
Crumlin Bowling Club - Tel: 4558142.
Cuala GAA Club - Tel: 2850783.
Garda Boat Club - Tel: 6770127.
Irish Hang Gliding Club - Tel: 4509845.
Irish Kennel Club - Tel: 4533300.
Irish Parachute Club - Tel: 4505448.
Irish Rowing Union - Tel: 4509831.
Junior Chamber IRE - Tel: 4963375.
Kilternan Tennis Centre - Tel: 2953720.
Lansdowne Football Club - Tel: 6689300.
Neptune Rowing Club - Tel: 6775079.

Pierrot Snooker Club - Tel: 8729631.
Polo Club - Tel: 6776248.
St. Brigids GAA - Tel: 8202484.
St. Mary's College RFC - Tel: 4900440.
St. Judes G.A.A. Club - Tel: 4905255
St. Vincent's Hurling & Football Club -
Tel: 8335722.
Ski Club of IRE - Tel: 2955658.
Stackstown Golf Club - Tel: 4942338.
Sutton Lawn Tennis - Tel: 8323035.
Terenure RFC - Tel: 4907572.

HELP AND ADVICE
SOCIAL SERVICE AND WELFARE
ORGANISATIONS
Adoption Board Tel: 6715888.
Aidlink Tel: 2887314.
Alcoholics Anonymous Tel: 4538998.
Asthma Society of Ireland Tel: 6716551.
Cherish Tel: 6682744.
Dr Barnardos Tel; 4530355.
Dublin Central Mission Tel: 8742123.
Irish Epilepsy Association Tel: 4557500.
Irish Heart Foundation Tel: 6685001.
Irish Red Cross Tel: 6765135.
*Irish Society for Prevention of Cruelty to
Children* Tel: 6794944.
Irish Wheelchair Association
Tel: 8338241.
National Association for the Deaf
Tel: 8388124.
National Council for the Blind
Tel: 8307033.
Rape Crisis Centre Tel: 6613923.
Rehabilition Institute Tel: 2698422.
Samaritans Tel: 8727700 - 1850609090
St Vincent De Paul Tel: 8384164.
Victim Support Tel: 6798673.

HOSPITALS
Beaumont Beaumont Road.
Tel: 8377755.
Blackrock Clinic Rock Road.
Tel: 2832222.
James Connolly Blanchardstown.
Tel: 8213844.
Mater Misericordiae Eccles Street.
Tel: 8301122.
Mater Private Eccles Street. Tel: 8384444.
Rotunda Hospital Parnell Square.
Tel: 8730700
St. James James Street. Tel: 4537941.
St. Laurence's (Richmond), North
Brunswick Street. Tel: 8720303.

St. Michaels Lower George Street, Dun
Laoghaire. Tel: 2806901.
St. Michaels (Pte) Crofton Road, Dun
Laoghaire. Tel: 2808411.
St. Patrick's Bow Lane West.
Tel: 6775423.
St. Vincents Elm Park. Tel: 2694533.

GARDA SIOCHANA (POLICE)
Dublin Metropolitan Area Headquarters,
Harcourt Square. Tel: 8732222.

EMBASSIES
American Tel: 6688777.
Apostolic Nunciature Tel: 8380577
Arab Republic of Egypt Tel: 6606566.
Australian Tel: 6761517.
British Tel: 2695211
Canadian Tel: 4781988.
French Tel: 2601666
German Tel: 2693011.
Italian Tel: 6601744.
Spanish Tel: 2691640.

CAR REPAIRS
Annesley Motor Company Ballybough.
Tel: 8723033.
Brady's (Dublin) Ltd Navan Road,
Castleknock. Tel: 8213053.
Carroll and Kinsella Motors Walkinstown
Road. Tel: 4508142.
Parkgate Motors Parkgate Street.
Tel: 6775677.

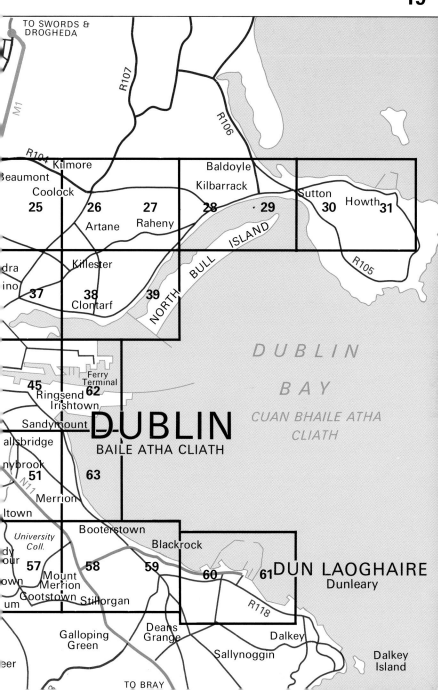

TO SWORDS & DROGHEDA

M1

R107

R106

R101

Kilmore

Beaumont

Coolock

Baldoyle

Kilbarrack

Sutton

Howth

25

26

27

28

29

30

31

Artane

Raheny

Killester

dra

ino

37

38

Clontarf

39

NORTH

BULL ISLAND

R105

D U B L I N

B A Y

Ferry Terminal

45

62

Ringsend

Irishtown

Sandymount

DUBLIN

BAILE ATHA CLIATH

CUAN BHAILE ATHA CLIATH

allsbridge

nybrook

N11

51

Merrion

ltown

63

Booterstown

Blackrock

University Coll.

dy

our

own

um

57

58

59

60

61

DUN LAOGHAIRE

Dunleary

Mount Merrion

Gootstown

Stillorgan

R118

eer

Galloping Green

Deans Grange

Dalkey

Sallynoggin

Dalkey Island

TO BRAY

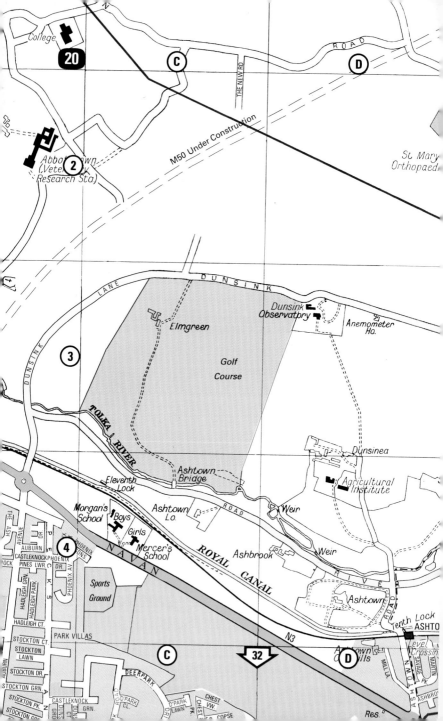

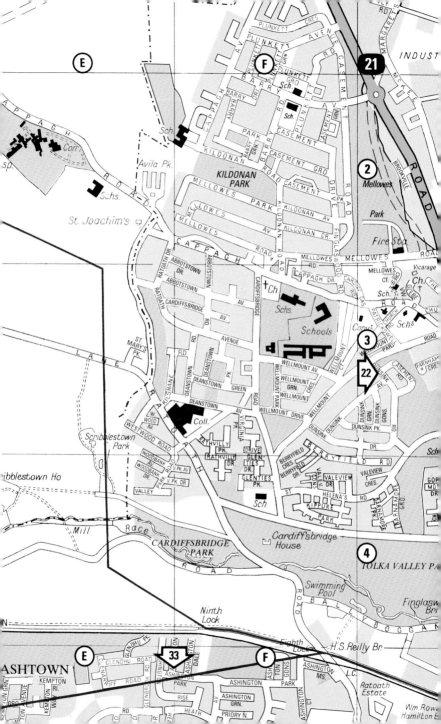

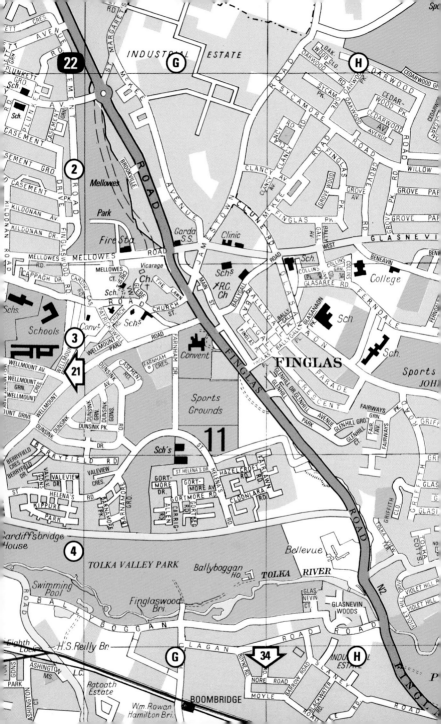

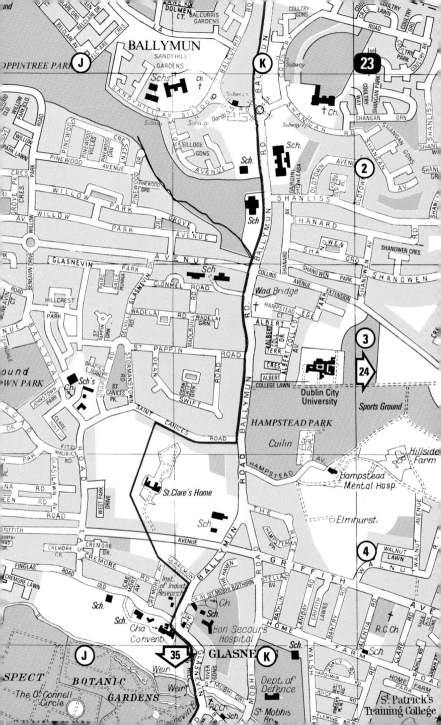

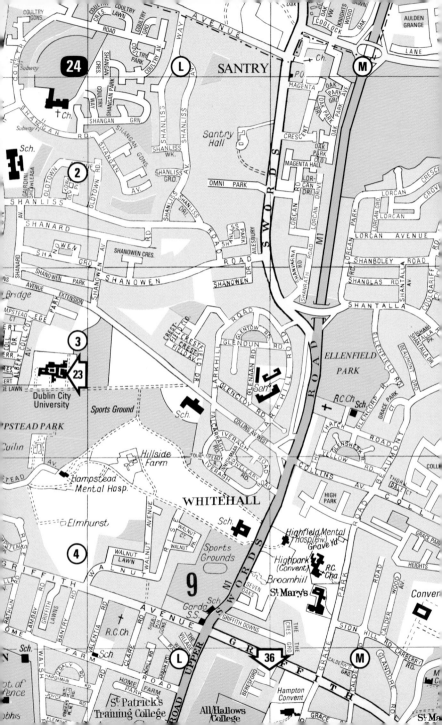

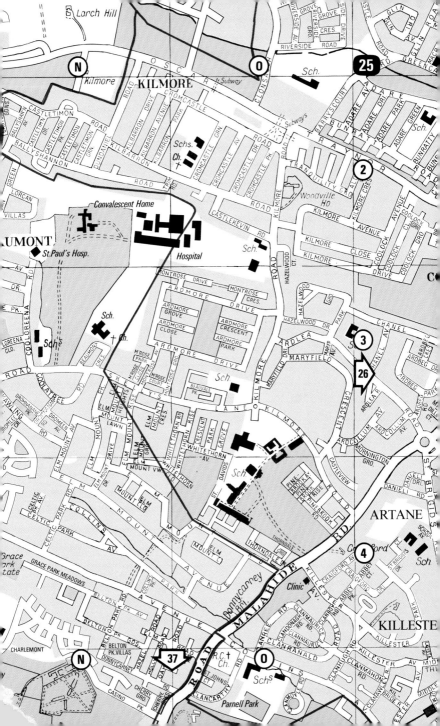

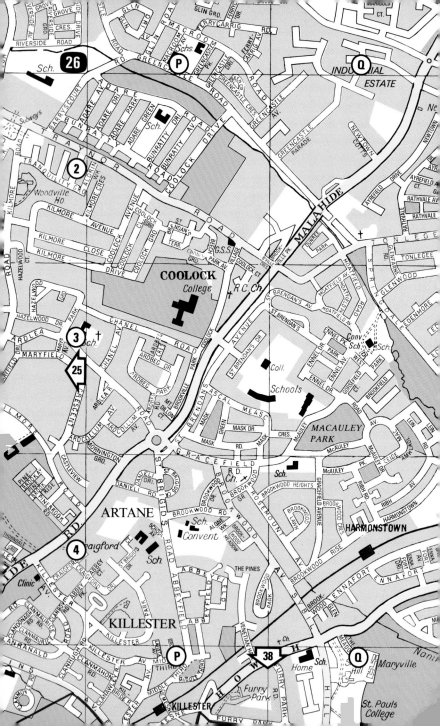

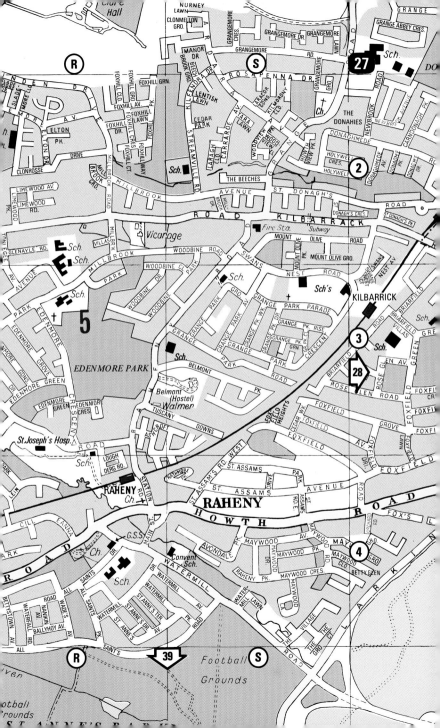

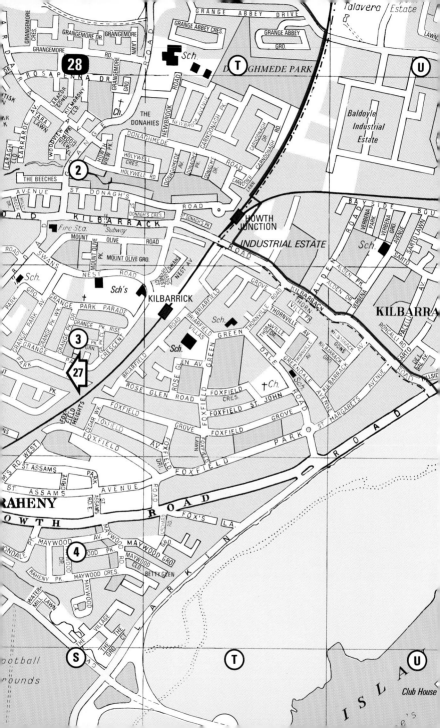

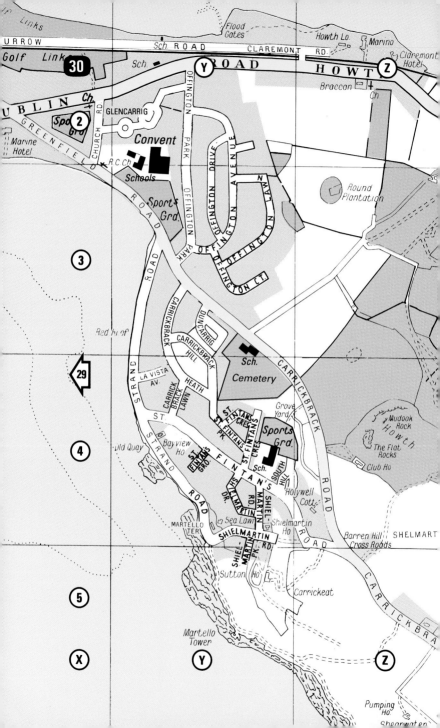

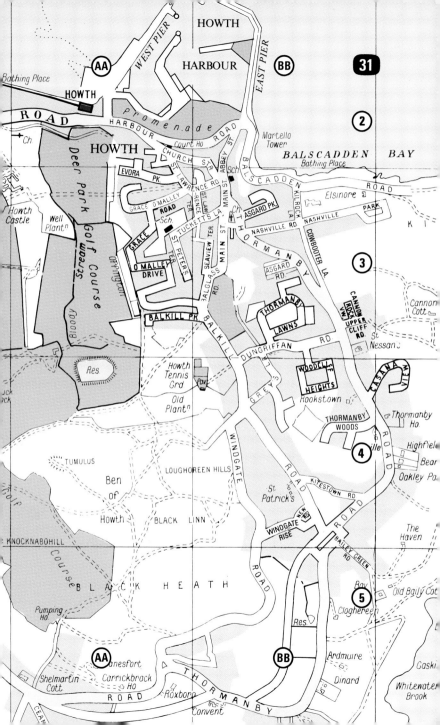

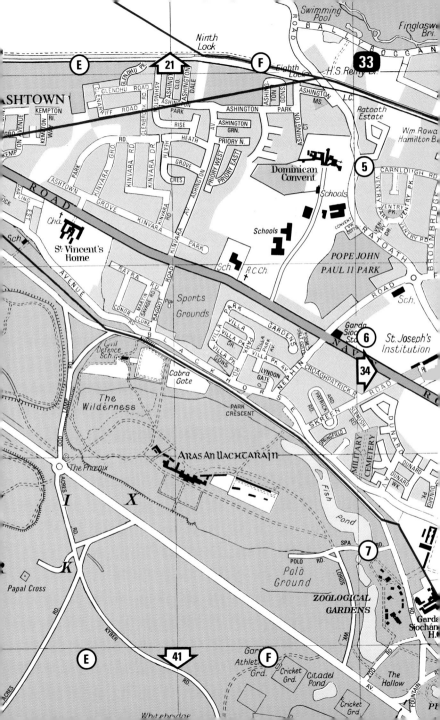

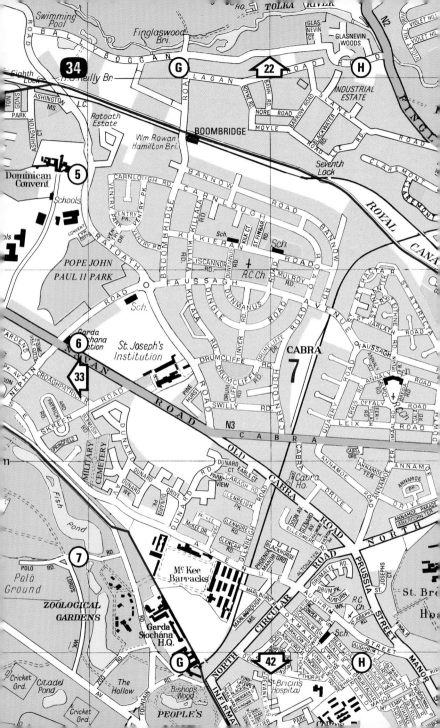

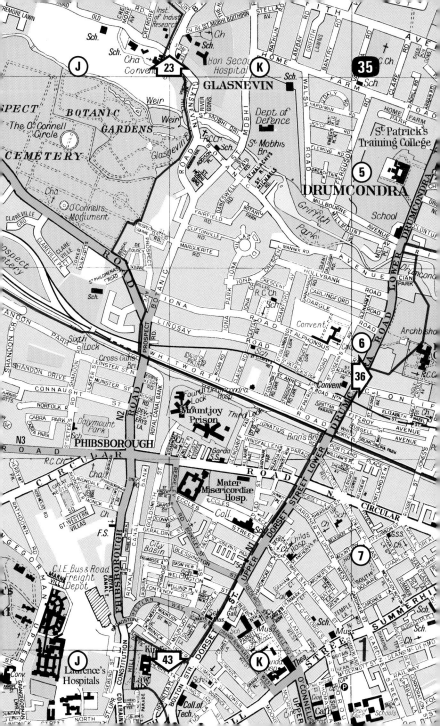

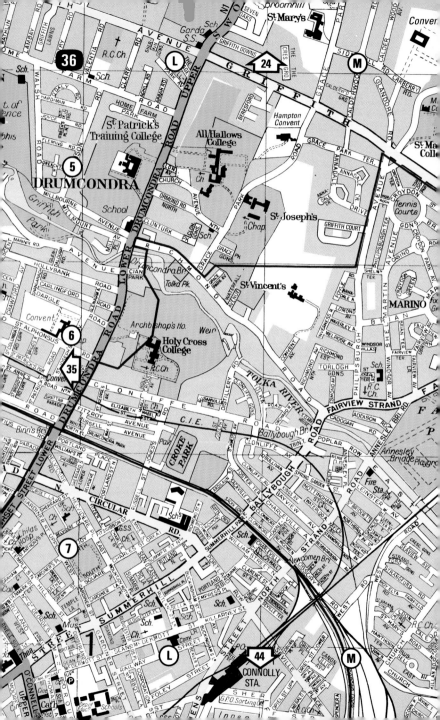

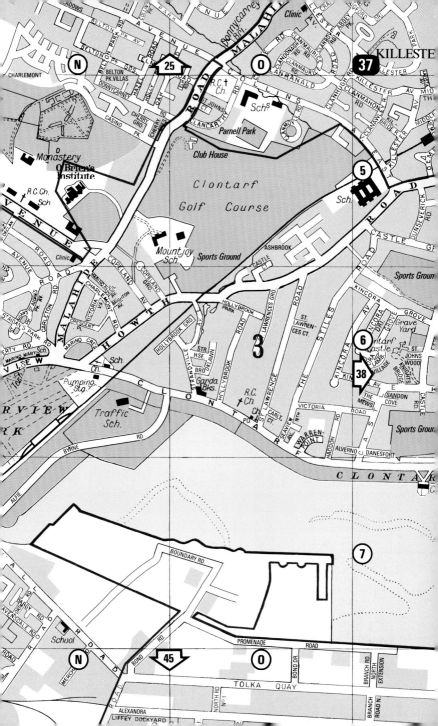

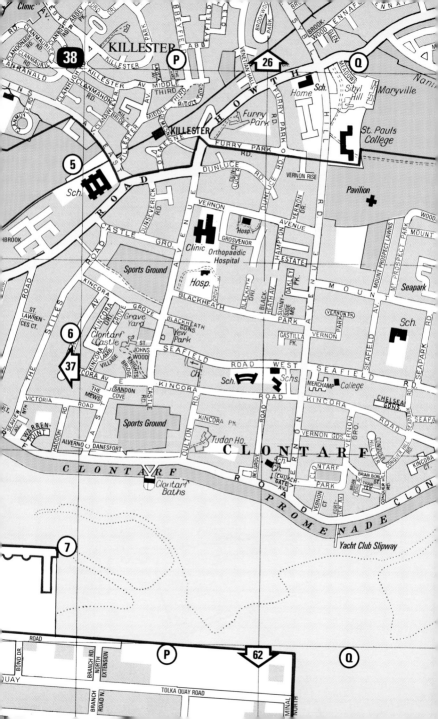

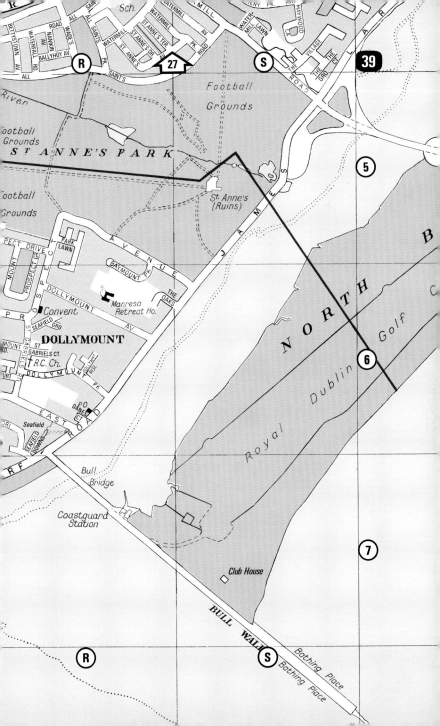

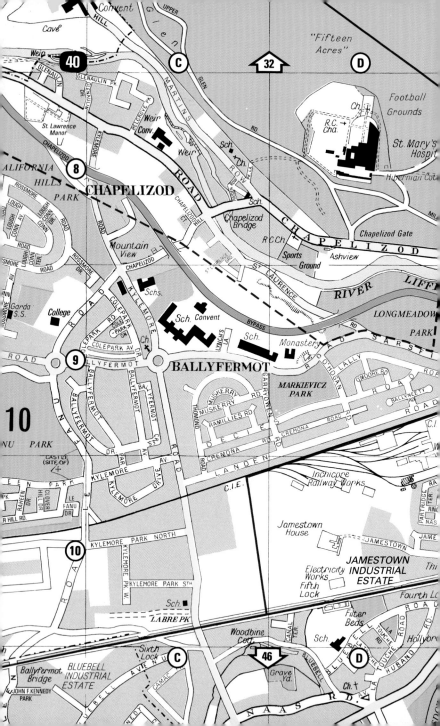

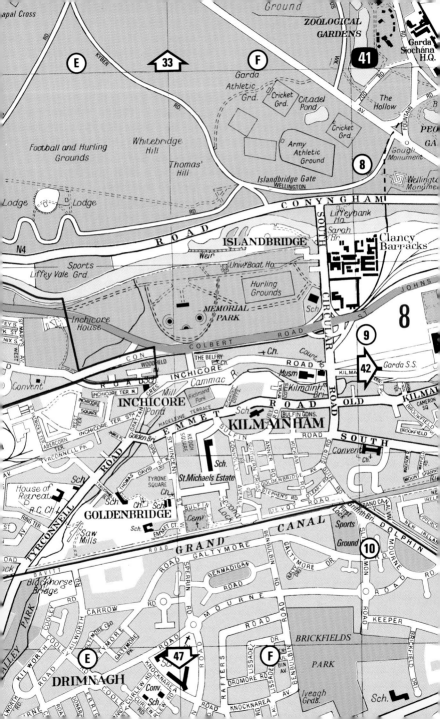

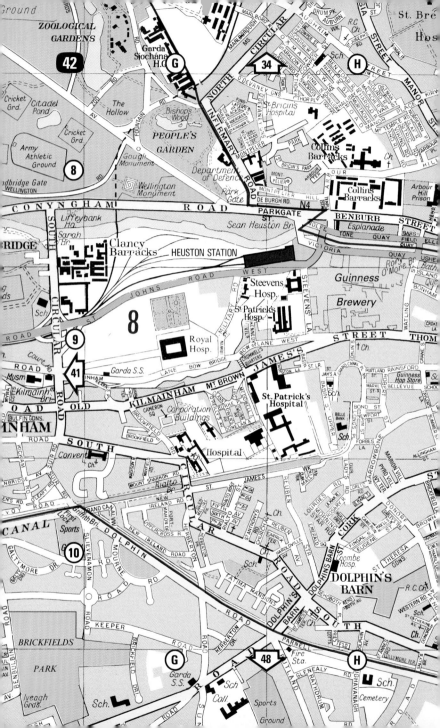

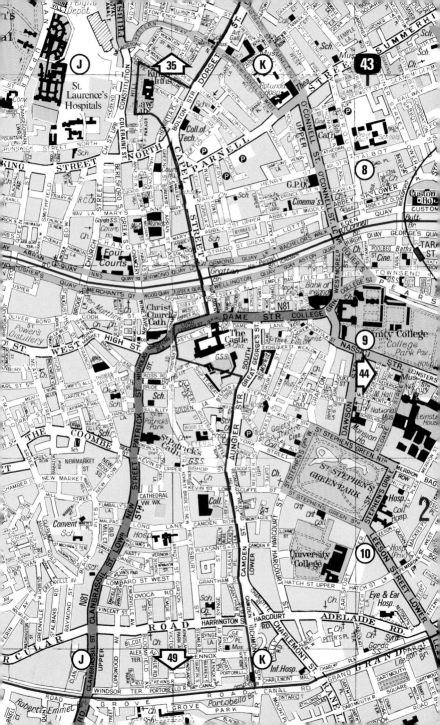

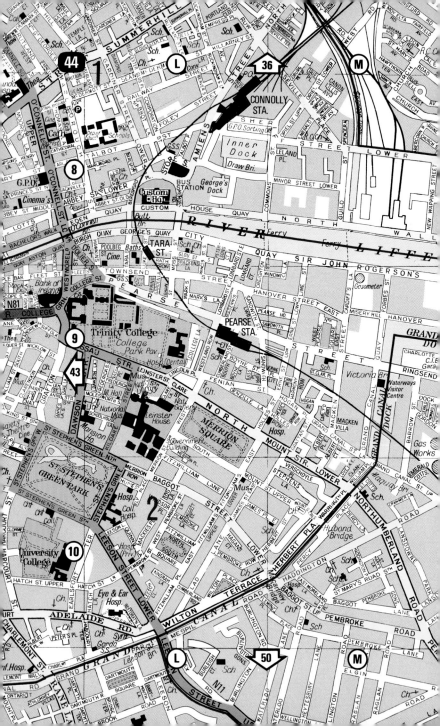

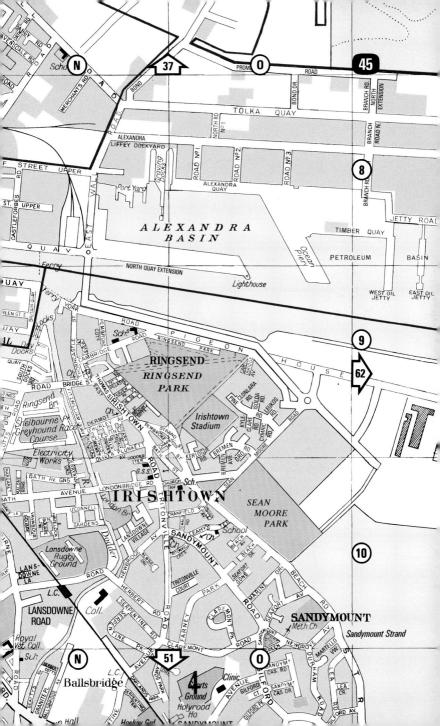

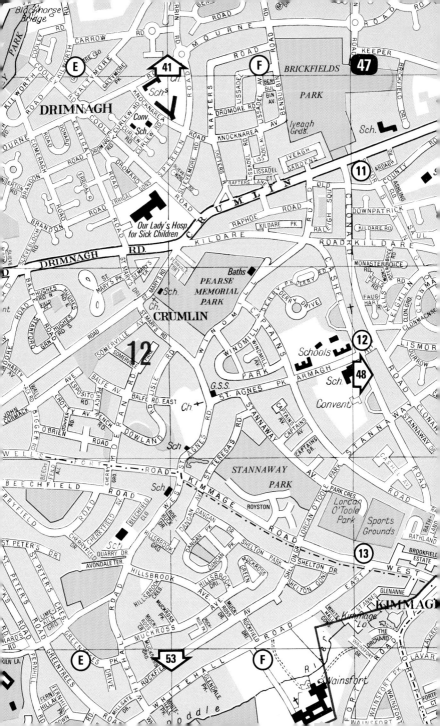

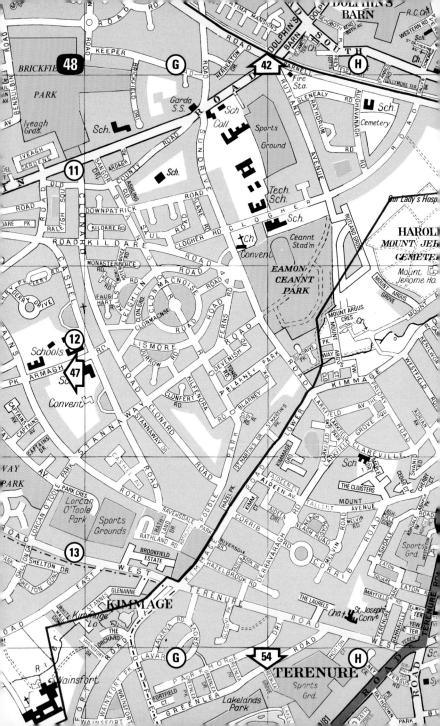

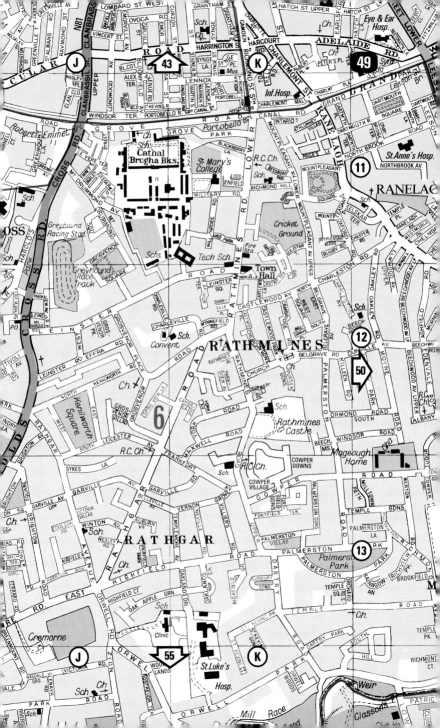

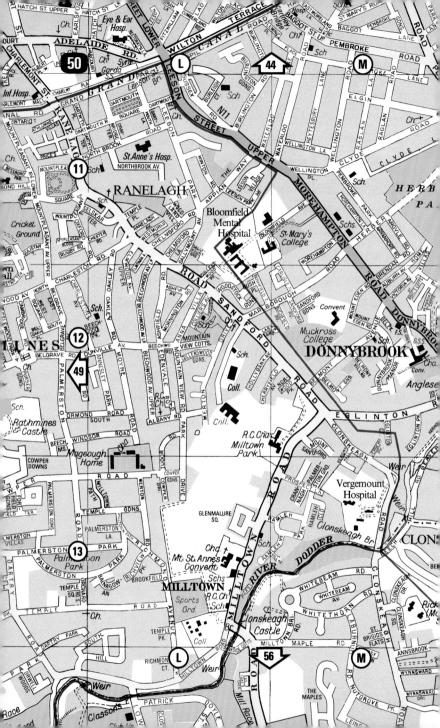

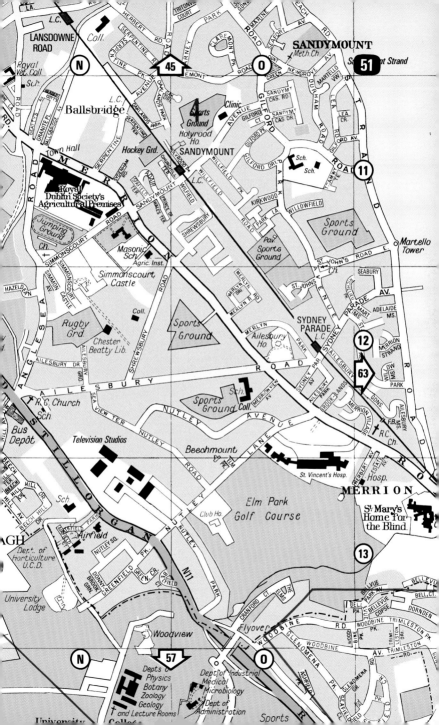

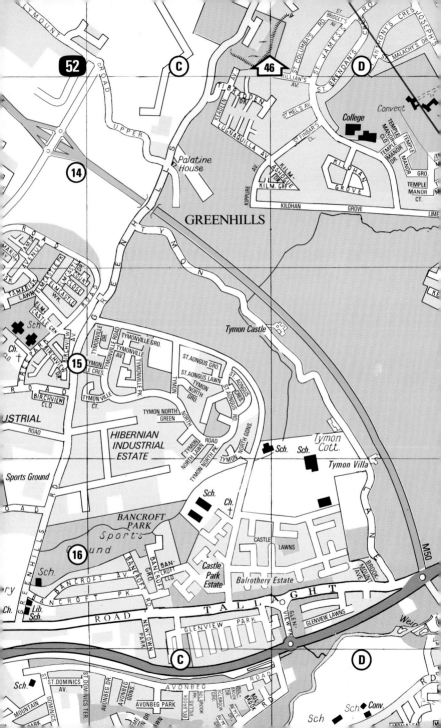

C

46

D

14

GREENHILLS

Palatine House

Convent

College

TEMPLE MANOR CLO.
TEMPLE MANOR DR.
TEMPLE MANOR

TEMPLE MANOR CT.

KILOHAN GROVE

KILM. ASHGR.
KILM. GRO.
KIPPURE AV.

KILOHAN GROVE

ST. BRIDGET'S AV.
ST. COLUMBA'S RD.
ST. JAMES'S RD.
ST. BRENDAN'S
ST. ANTHONY'S CRES.
ST. JOSEPH'S
ST. MALACHY'S DR.

LILLIAN'S AV.
ST. MEL'S AV.
ST. FINBAR'S CL.

TIBRADDEN DR.
KLADEN DR.
LUGNAQUILLA AV.

UPPER

ROAD

15

16

Tymon Castle

TYMONVILLE DR.
TYMONVILLE ROAD
TYMONVILLE AV.
TYMONVILLE GRO.
TYMONVILLE PK.
TYMONVILLE CRES.
TYMONVILLE CT.

ST. AONGUS GRO.
ST. AONGUS LAWN
ST. AONGUS
ST. AONGUS CRES.
ST. AONGUS RD.

TYMON NORTH GRO.
TYMON NORTH GREEN
TYMON NORTH ROAD
TYMON NORTH LAWN
TYMON NORTH PK.
TYMON NORTH GDNS.

TYMON
NORTH

HIBERNIAN INDUSTRIAL ESTATE

USTRIAL

ROAD

TAMARISK
TAMARISK AVENUE
TAMARISK LAWN
ELMCASTLE COURT
ELMCASTLE CLOSE
ELMCASTLE WK.
ELM. CASTLE GRN.
ELMCASTLE DR.
Sch.
Ch.
CLO.
BIRCHVIEW AV.
BIRCHVIEW DR.
BIRCHVIEW CLO.

Sch.
Sch.

Tymon Cott.

Tymon Villa

Sports Ground

Sch.
Ch.

BANCROFT PARK
Sports Ground

BANCROFT AV.
BANCROFT GRO.
BANCROFT CLO.
BAN. CROFT

Castle Park Estate

CASTLE LAWNS

Balrothery Estate

BROOK MOUNT AVE.

M50

Sch.
Ch.
Lib.
Sch.

GREENHILLS ROAD

BANCROFT PK.

NEWTOWN PARK

GLENVIEW PARK

GLEN-VIEW RD.

GLENVIEW LAWNS

TALLAGHT

Weir

C

D

Sch.
ST. DOMINICS AV.
ST. DOMINICS TER.
ST. DOMINICS DR.
AVONBEG DR.
AVONBEG GDNS.
AVONBEG
AVONBEG PARK
MOUNTAIN

BOLBROOK DR.
BOLBROOK GRO.
BOLBROOK AV.
BOLBROOK

Sch.
Sch. Conv.
Sch.

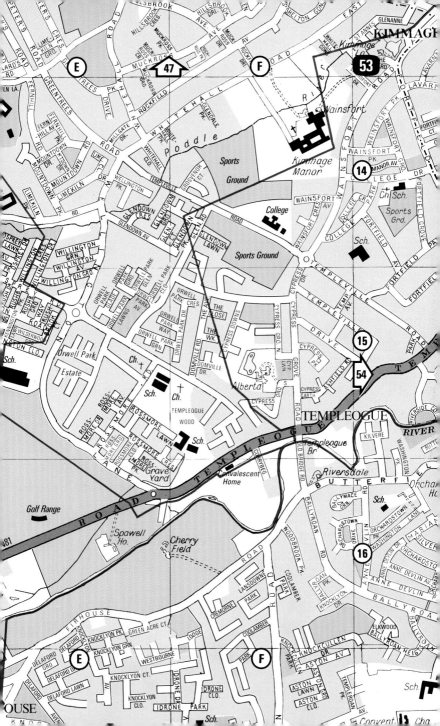

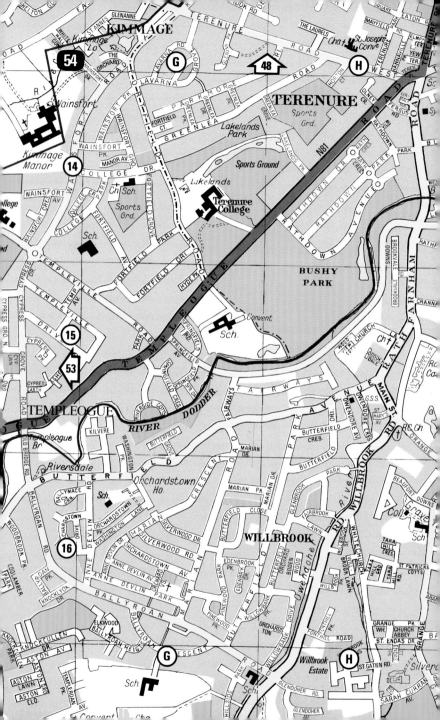

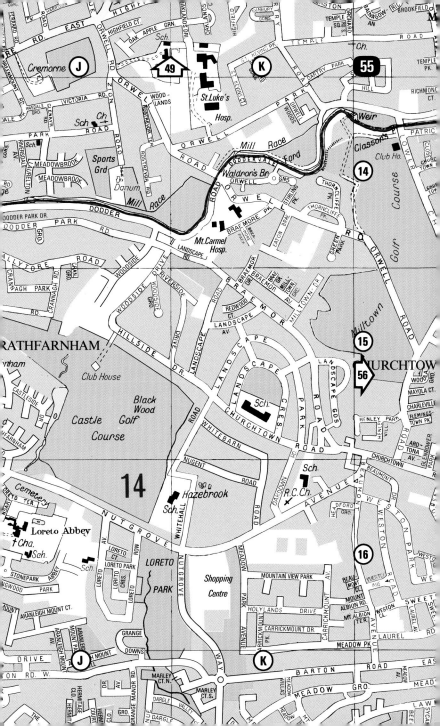

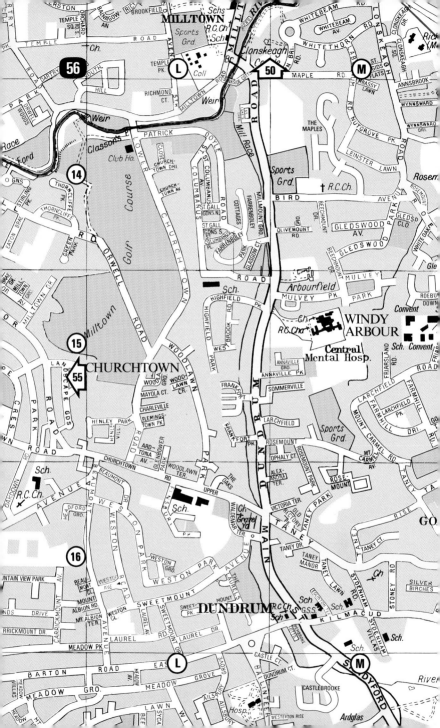

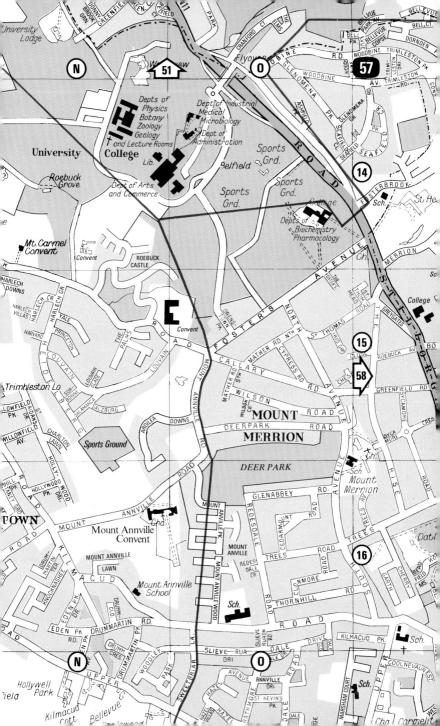

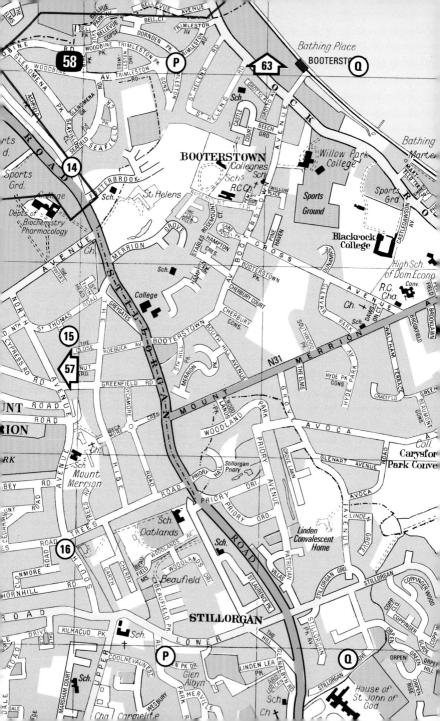

T

U

14

Bathing Places

SEAPOINT

N31

15

Baths

NEWTOWN AV

SEAPOINT

ERCILIE PK

CRES

TEMPLE

AVENUE

Bathing Places
Martello
Tower

BRIGHTON VALE

BRIGHTON VALE RD

SEAPOINT

St.Patrick's
Infant Hosp.

TRAFALGAR TER

TRAFALGAR LA

EATON PL NORTH

BELGRAVE

BELGRAVE RD

ALMA

ROAD

MONKS

TEMPLE HILL

MONTPL
PL

SHANDON PK

CLELLIER
PAR

59

TOWN

EATON
SQ

EATON PL
SOUTH

BELGRAVE SQ

SEAFIELD

Sch

BELGRAVE PL

SEAPOINT

ALBANY

AVENUE

CLIFTON LA

BRIGHTON

ROAD

CLIFTON
AV

CLIFTON

ALMA

Jetties

SALTHILL &
MONKSTOWN

Sch

Old Harbour

Dunlear
Pier

WE

LONGFORD

N31

TERRACE

LONGFORD

MONKSTOWN CR.

OLD DUNLEARY

DUNLEARY ROAD

DUNLEARY
HILL

CUMBERLAND
STR.

Sch

BARRETT
ST.

SMITH
VS.

WIL
LOW
BANK

CLAREN

AVENUE HILL

MONKS
TOWN
HILL

De Vesci
Gardens

SLOPERTON

VESEY
PL

VESEY GDNS

PLACE

GREENVILLE RD.

STRADBROOK
LAWN

STRADBROOK
PK.

STRAD
BROOK
GDNS.

QUEENS PARK

GLEANN
NA SMOL

THE WILLOWS

THE MAPLES

THE CEDARS

THE ALDERS

THE
POPLARS

MONKSTOWN
VALLEY

MONKSTOWN

Sch

CARRICKBRENNAN

R.C.Ch.

Ch.

PAKENHAM

Monkstown
Hosp.

DUN LAOGHAIRE
(Dunleary)

Sch

Ch.

TIVOLI

Cha

OAK
LAW

BROOKLAWN AV

ILLE

CRESCENT

STRADBROOK

16

radbrook

WYNBERG PK.

WYNBERG
AV

Sports

Ground

RICHMOND
PK.

Richmond Hill

CARRICK
BRENNAN LAWN

RICHMOND

PK.

BROOK PARK

ASHTON
PK.

RICHMOND
GRO

Monkstown
Park

Sch

AVO

MOUNT
TOWN

UPPER

ST. JOHN'S PK

Ch.

Y

O

TIVOLI TC

TIVOLI

OWANBYRN

ROWAN PK.
AV

ROCKFORD PK.

ROCKFORD PARK

Convent

WINDSOR
PARK

WINDSOR DR.

ASHTON
PARK

ASHTON PK.

MONKSTOWN
GRO

Castle

CASTLE PARK

Dunedin

Monkstown
Ho.

DUNEDIN TER

Castle

MOUNT WOOD

GLANDORE
PK.

WOOD LC

HIGH TOWER

BROOKVILLE
PARK

SPRINGHILL
PK.

SPRINGHILL

17

STRADBROOK RD

STRADBROOK
HILL

Sports Grd.

ABBEY
PK.

LANESVILLE

MONKSTOWN
FM. TER

O.PLUNKETT
TER

SAINT
CLO.
PATRICK'S
CRESCENT

OLIVER
PLUNKETT

Fitzgerald
Park

PAT.
RICTAL
GDNS.

MOUNT
TOWN
LOWER

MOUNT TOWN

HIGH TOWER RD

S

ST FINTAN'S
PARK

ST FINTAN'S
CLO

RORY
O'CONNOR
CT

ABBEY
VW.

CASEMENT
PARK

T

OLIVER PLUNKETT

ABBEY
PK.

OLIVER
PLUNK
ETT

ROSE
PARK

BIRCHGROVE

ASHGROVE

AVENUE

PATRICIAN
PK.

CARRICK
BRE
GDNS

U

Hi

Deans Grange
Cemetery

ST FINTAN'S RD

KILL ABBEY

GLENAGEARY

POLF

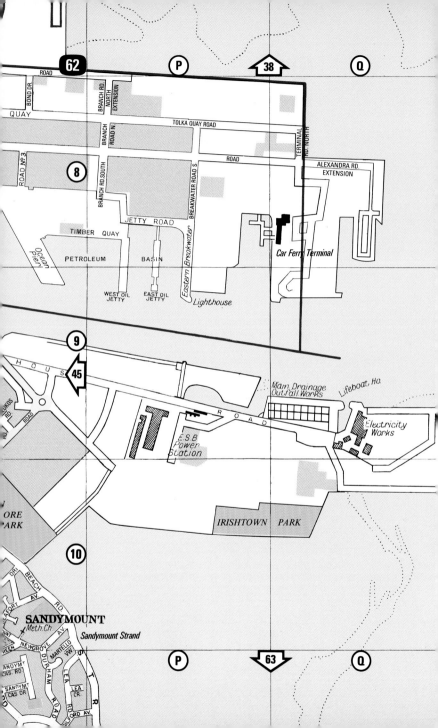

62
ROAD
P
38
Q

BOND DR.
BRANCH RD. NORTH EXTENSION

QUAY
BRANCH ROAD N.
TOLKA QUAY ROAD

ROAD No. 3
8
BRANCH RD. SOUTH
ROAD
ALEXANDRA RD. EXTENSION

TERMINAL ROAD NORTH

BREAKWATER ROAD S.

JETTY ROAD

TIMBER QUAY

Ocean Pier
PETROLEUM
BASIN

Eastern Breakwater
Car Ferry Terminal

WEST OIL JETTY
EAST OIL JETTY
Lighthouse

9

HOUS
45

ROAD

Main Drainage Outfall Works
Lifeboat Ho.

E.S.B. Power Station
Electricity Works

IRISHTOWN PARK

10

DRI.
BEACH AV.

SANDYMOUNT
Meth.Ch.
Sandymount Strand

NEWGROVE AV.
DURHAM
MARTELLO VW.

SANDYMT. CAS. RD.
LEA CR.
LEA RD.
ILFORD AV.
ROAD

P
63
Q

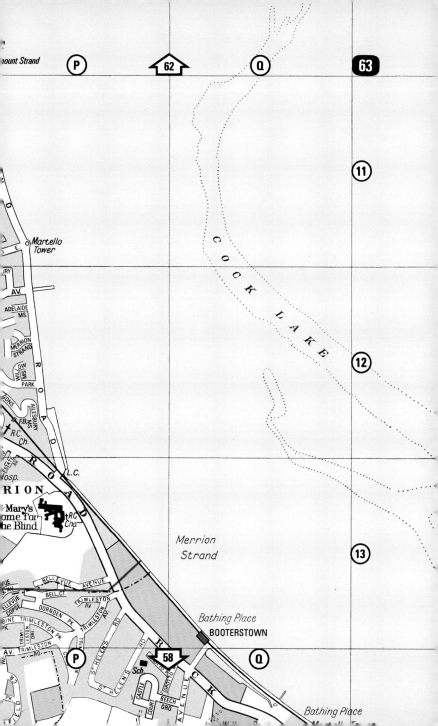

nount Strand

P

62

Q

63

11

Martello
Tower

JRY

AV.

ADELAIDE
MS.

MERRION
STRAND

WILLOW
PARK

C O C K   L A K E

DNS

AILESBURY

F.B. MS.

RC.
Ch.

12

ROAD

L.C.

osp.

R I O N

Mary's
ome for
he Blind

RC
Cha

Merrion
Strand

13

BELLEVUE   AVENUE

BELL CT.

BELLEVUE
COPSE

DORNDEN PK.

TRIMLESTON
AV.

BINE TRIMLESTON PK.

TRIM-
LESTON
RD.

TRIMLESTON AV.

AV. TRIMLESTON
RD.

ROCK

Bathing Place

BOOTERSTOWN

P

58

Q

ST HELENS   RD.

ST HELENS   RD.

CASTLE
COURT

Sch.

GROTTO

BEECH
GRO.

AVENUE

Bathing Place

INDEX TO STREETS

General Abbreviations

Av.	Avenue	Gdn.	Garden	Pl.	Place
Bk.	Bank	Gdns.	Gardens	Prom.	Promenade
Bldgs.	Buildings	Gra.	Grange	Rd.	Road
Boul.	Boulevard	Grd.	Ground	Rds.	Roads
Bri.	Bridge	Grn.	Green	Ri.	Rise
Cem.	Cemetery	Gro.	Grove	S.	South
Ch.	Church	Ho.	House	Sch.	School
Clo.	Close	Hosp.	Hospital	Sq.	Square
Coll.	College	La.	Lane	St.	Street
Cotts.	Cottages	Lo.	Lodge	Sta.	Station
Cres.	Crescent	Lwr.	Lower	Ter.	Terrace
Ct.	Court	Mans.	Mansions	Vill.	Villa
Dr.	Drive	Mkt.	Market	Vills.	Villas
E.	East	Ms.	Mews	Vw.	View
Est.	Estate	Mt.	Mount	W.	West
Ex.	Exchange	N.	North	Wd.	Wood
Ext.	Extension	No.	Numbers	Wds.	Woods
Fld.	Field	Par.	Parade	Wk.	Walk
Flds.	Fields	Pas.	Passage	Yd.	Yard
Fm.	Farm	Pk.	Park		

District Abbreviations

D.L.   Dún Laoghaire

Notes

This index contains some street names in standard text which are followed by another street named in italics. In these cases the street in standard text does not actually appear on the map due to insufficient space but can be located close to the street named in italics.

Name	Ref
Arranmore Av. 7	35 K6
Arranmore Rd. 4	50 M11
Arus An Uactarian 8	33 F6
Ascal An Charrain Chno (Nutgrove Av.) 14	55 J16
Ascal Bhaile An Abba (Abbotstown Av.) 11	21 F3
Ascal Mac Amhlaoi (McAuley Av.) 5	26 Q3
Ascal Measc (Mask Av.) 5	26 P3
Ascal Ratabhachta (Rathoath Av.) 11	21 E3
Asgard Pk., Howth	31 BB3
Asgard Rd., Howth	31 BB3
Ash St. 8	43 J9
Ashbrook 3	37 O5
Ashbrook 7	33 E5
Ashbrook, Castleknock	32 D5
Ashcroft 5	27 R3
Ashdale Av. 6	48 H13
Ashdale Gdns. 6	48 H13
Ashdale Pk. 6	48 H13
Ashdale Rd. 6	48 H13
Ashfield Av. 6	50 L12
Ashfield Clo. 6	53 F15
Ashfield Rd.	
Ashfield Pk. (Templeogue) 6	53 F15
Ashfield Rd.	
Ashfield Pk. (Terenure) 6	48 H13
Ashfield Pk., Booterstown	57 O14
Ashfield Rd. (Ranelagh) 6	50 L12
Ashfield Rd. (Templeogue) 6	53 F15
Ashford Cotts. 7	34 H7
Ashford St.	
Ashford Pl. 7	34 H7
Ashford St.	
Ashford St. 7	34 H7
Ashgrove, D.L.	60 T17
Ashington Av. 7	33 F5
Ashington Clo. 7	33 E5
Ashington Ct. 7	33 F5
Ashington Dale 7	33 E5
Ashington Gdns. 7	33 F5
Ashington Grn. 7	33 E5
Ashington Ms. 7	33 F5
Ashington Pk. 7	33 E5
Ashington Ri. 7	33 E5
Ashling Clo. 12	48 G11
Ashton Pk., D.L.	60 L7
Ashtown Gate Rd. 8	32 D5
Ashtown Gro. 7	33 E5
Ashtown Rd., Castleknock	32 D5
Ashtown Sta., Castleknock	20 D4
Aston Pl. 2	43 K8
Aston Quay 2	43 K8
Athlumney Vills. 6	49 K11
Auburn Av. 4	50 M12
Auburn Rd. 4	50 M12
Auburn Av.	
Auburn St. 7	35 J7
Auburn Vills. 6	49 J13
Auburn Wk. 7	34 H7
Audilaun Rd. 3	36 L7
Aughavanagh Rd. 12	48 H11
Aughrim La. 7	34 H7
Aughrim Pl. 7	34 H7
Aughrim St. 7	34 H7
Aughrim Vills. 7	34 H7
Aughrim St.	
Aungier Pl. 2	43 K9
Aungier St. 2	43 K9
Austins Cotts. 3	36 M7
Annesley Pl.	
Ave Maria Rd. 8	42 H10
Avenue, The 12	53 F15
Avenue Rd. 8	49 J11
Avoca Av., D.L.	58 Q15
Avoca Pl., D.L.	59 R15
Avoca Rd., D.L.	58 Q16
Avondale Av. 7	35 J7
Avondale Lawn, D.L.	59 R16
Avondale Lawn Ext., D.L.	59 R16
Avondale Pk. 5	27 S4
Avondale Rd. 7	35 J7
Avondale Ter. 12	47 E13
Ayrefield Av. 5	26 Q2
Ayrefield Ct. 5	26 Q2
Ayrefield Dr. 5	26 Q2
Ayrefield Gro. 5	26 Q2
Ayrefield Pl. 5	26 Q2
Bachelors Wk. 1	43 K8
Back La. 8	43 J9
Baggot Ct. 2	44 L10
Baggot La. 4	44 M10
Baggot Rd. 7	33 E6
Baggot St. Lwr. 2	44 L10
Baggot St. Upper 4	44 M10
Baggot Ter. 7	33 E6
Blackhorse Av.	
Bailey Grn. Rd., Howth	31 BB4
Baldoyle Rd., Baldoyle	29 W2
Balfe Av. 12	47 E12
Balfe Rd. 12	47 E12
Balfe Rd. E. 12	47 E12
Balfe St. 2	43 K9
Chatham St.	
Balglass Rd., Howth	31 BB3
Balkill Pk., Howth	31 AA3
Balkill Rd., Howth	31 BB3
Ballsbridge Av. 4	51 N11
Ballsbridge Ter. 4	51 N11
Ballsbridge Av.	
Ballyboggan Rd. 11	21 F4
Ballybough Av. 3	36 M7
Spring Gdn. St.	
Ballybough Bri. 3	36 M6
Ballybough Cotts. 3	36 M6
Ballybough Ct. 3	36 M7
Spring Gdn. St.	
Ballybough Rd. 3	36 M7
Ballyfermot Av. 10	40 C9
Ballyfermot Cres. 10	40 C9
Ballyfermot Hill 10	40 C8
Ballyfermot Par. 10	40 C9
Ballygall Av. 11	22 H2
Ballygall Cres. 11	22 G3
Ballygall Par. 11	22 G3
Ballygall Pl. 11	22 H3
Ballygall Rd. E. 11	23 J3
Ballygall Rd. W. 11	22 G3
Ballygihen Av., D.L.	61 W17
Ballyhoy Av. (Ascal Bhaile Thuaidh) 5	27 R4
Ballymace Grn. 14	53 F16
Ballymount Dr. 12	46 C13
Ballyneety Rd. 10	40 D9
Ballyroan Cres. 14	54 G16
Ballyroan Heights 14	54 G16
Ballyroan Pk. 14	53 F16
Ballyroan Rd. 14	53 F16
Ballyshannon Av. 5	25 N2
Ballyshannon Rd. 5	25 N2
Ballytore Rd. 14	55 J14
Balnagowan 6	50 L13
Balscadden Rd., Howth	31 BB3
Bancroft Clo., Tallaght	52 C16
Bancroft Gro., Tallaght	52 C16
Bancroft Rd., Tallaght	52 C16
Bangor Dr. 12	48 G11
Bangor Rd. 12	48 G11
Bank of Ireland 2	43 K9
Bankside Cotts. 14	56 L14
Bann Rd. 11	34 G5
Bannow Rd. 7	34 G5
Bantry Rd. 9	23 K4
Barclay Ct., D.L.	59 R15
Bargy Rd. 3	37 N7
Barnamore Cres. 11	22 G4
Barnamore Gro.	
Barnamore Gro. 11	22 G4
Barnamore Pk. 11	22 G4
Barrack St. 11	22 G3
Barrett St., D.L.	60 U16
Barrow Rd. 11	34 H5
Barrow St. 4	44 M9
Barry Av. 11	21 F2
Barry Dr. 11	21 F2
Barry Grn. 1	21 F2
Barry Pk. 11	21 F2
Barry Rd. 11	21 F2
Barryscourt Rd. 5	25 O2
Barton Dr. 14	54 H16
Basin St. Lwr. 8	42 H9
Basin St. Upper 8	42 H9
Basin Vw. Ter. 7	35 K7
Bass Pl. 2	44 L9
Bath Av. 4	45 N10
Bath Av. Gdns. 4	45 N10
Bath Av. Pl. 4	45 N10
Bath La. 1	35 K7
Bath Pl., D.L.	59 R15
Bath St. 4	45 N9
Baymount Pk. 3	39 R6
Bayside Boul. N., Kilbarrack	28 U2
Bayside Pk., Kilbarrack	28 U2
Bayside Sq. E., Kilbarrack	29 U2
Bayside Sq. N., Kilbarrack	29 U2
Bayside Sq. S., Kilbarrack	29 U3
Bayside Sq. W., Kilbarrack	29 U3
Bayside Wk., Kilbarrack	28 U2
Bayview 4	45 N9
Pembroke St.	
Bayview Av. 3	36 M7
Beach Av. 4	45 O10
Beach Dr. 4	45 O10
Beach Rd. 4	45 O10
Beach Vw., Howth	28 U3
Beaconsfield Ct. 8	41 F9
The Belfry	
Beattys Av. 4	51 N11
Beaufield Ms., D.L.	58 P16
Beaufield Pk., Stillorgan	58 P16
Beaufort, D.L.	61 W17
Beaufort Downs 14	54 H16
Beaumont Av. 14	56 L16
Beaumont Clo. 14	55 K16
Beaumont Cres. 9	25 N3
Beaumont Dr. 14	56 L16
Beaumont Gro. 9	24 M3
Beaumont Rd. 9	24 M4
Beauvale Pk. 5	25 O3
Beaver Row 4	50 M13
Beaver St. 1	44 L8
Bedford Row 2	43 K9
Temple Bar	
Beech Gro., D.L.	58 Q14
Beech Hill 4	50 M13
Beech Hill Av. 4	51 N13
Beech Hill Cres. 4	51 N13
Beech Hill Dr. 4	51 N13
Beech Hill Ter. 4	51 N13
Beech Hill Vills. 4	51 N13
Beech Hill Ter.	
Beech Pk. Av. 5	26 P2
Beechdale Ms. 6	49 K12
Beeches, The 5	27 S2
Beechfield Av. 12	47 E13
Beechfield Clo. 12	47 E13
Beechfield Rd. 12	47 E13
Beechmount Dr. 14	56 M14
Beechwood Av. Lwr.6	50 L12
Beechwood Av. Upper 6	50 L12
Beechwood Pk. 6	49 K12
Beechwood Pk., D.L.	61 V17
Beechwood Rd. 6	50 L12
Beggarsbush Barracks 4	44 M10
Belfield Ct. 4	51 N13
Belfield Downs 4	56 M15
Belfry, The 8	41 F9
Belgrave Av. 6	49 K12
Belgrave Pl. 6	49 K12
Belgrave Rd. 6	49 K12
Belgrave Rd., D.L.	59 S15
Belgrave Sq. E. 6	49 K12
Belgrave Sq. E., D.L.	60 T15
Belgrave Sq. N. 6	49 K12
Belgrave Sq. N., D.L.	59 S15
Belgrave Sq. S. 6	49 K12
Belgrave Sq. S., D.L.	59 S15
Belgrave Sq. W. 6	49 K12
Belgrave Sq. W., D.L.	59 S15
Belgrave Ter., D.L.	59 S15
Belgrove Lawn, Chapelizod	40 C8
Belgrove Rd., Chapelizod	40 C8
Bella Av. 1	36 L7
Bella St.	
Bella St. 1	36 L7
Belle Bk. 8	42 H9
Belleville Av. 6	49 J13
Bellevue 8	42 H9
Bellevue Av. 4	63 P13
Bellevue Copse, D.L.	63 P13
Bellevue Ct., D.L.	63 P13
Bellevue Pk., Stillorgan	63 P13
Bellevue Pk. Av., D.L.	63 P13
Belmont Av. 4	50 M12
Belmont Ct. 4	50 M12
Belmont Av.	
Belmont Gdns. 4	50 M12
Belmont Pk. 4	50 M12
Belmont Pk. 5	27 S3
Belmont Vills. 4	50 M12
Belton Pk. Av. 9	25 N4
Belton Pk. Gdns. 9	25 N4
Belton Pk. Rd. 9	25 N4
Belton Pk. Vills. 9	37 N5
Belvedere Av. 1	36 L7
Belvedere Ct. 1	35 K7
Belvedere Pl. 1	35 K7
Belvedere Rd. 1	35 K7
Belview Bldgs. 8	42 H9
School St.	
Ben Edar Rd. 7	34 H7
Ben Inagh Pk., Booterstown	59 R14
Benbulbin Av. 12	47 F11
Benbulbin Rd. 12	41 F10
Benburb St. 7	42 H8
Beneavin Ct. 11	23 J3
Beneavin Dr. 11	23 J3
Beneavin Pk. 11	22 H2
Beneavin Rd. 11	22 H2
Bengal Ter. 9	35 J5
Benmadigan Rd. 12	41 F10
Benson St. 2	45 N9
Beresford 9	36 L5
Beresford La. 1	44 L8
Beresford Pl. 1	44 L8
Beresford St. 7	43 J8
Berkeley Rd. 7	35 K7
Berkeley St. 7	35 K7
Berkeley Ter. 4	45 N10
Berryfield Cres. 11	21 F3
Berryfield Dr. 11	21 F3
Berryfield Rd. 11	21 F3
Berystede 6	50 L11
Leeson Pk.	
Bessborough Av. 3	36 M7

Name	Ref	Name	Ref	Name	Ref	Name	Ref
Bessborough Par. 6	49 K11	Bow La. W. 8	42 G9	Brookwood Cres. 5	26 Q4	Camden Mkt. 2	43 K10
Bethesda Pl. 1	35 K7	Bow St. 7	43 J8	Brookwood Dr. 5	26 P4	*Camden St. Lwr.*	
Dorset St. Upper		Boyne La. 2	44 L9	Brookwood Glen 5	26 Q4	Camden Pl. 2	43 K10
Bettyglen 5	28 T4	Boyne Rd. 11	34 G5	Brookwood Gro. 5	26 P4	Camden Row 8	43 K10
Bettystown Av. 5	27 R4	Boyne St. 2	44 L9	Brookwood Heights 5	26 P4	Camden St. Lwr. 2	43 K10
Big Bri. 6	54 H14	Brabazon Row 8	43 J10	Brookwood Lawn 5	26 Q4	Camden St. Upper 2	43 K10
Bigger Rd. 12	47 E12	Brabazon Sq. 8	43 J9	Brookwood	26 P4	Cameron Sq. 8	42 G9
Binn Eadair Vw.,	29 W2	*Pimlico*		Meadow 5		Cameron St. 8	42 H10
Sutton		Brabazon St. 8	43 J9	Brookwood Pk. 5	26 P4	Campbells Row 1	36 L7
Binns Bri. 1	35 K6	Brackens La. 2	44 L8	Brookwood Ri. 5	26 Q4	*Portland St. N.*	
Birchfield 14	57 N16	Braemor Av. 14	55 K15	Brookwood Rd. 5	26 P4	Canal Rd. 6	49 K11
Birchgrove, D.L.	60 T17	Braemor Dr. 14	55 K15	Broombridge Rd. 7	34 G5	Canal Ter. 12	40 D10
Birchs La. 14	56 M16	Braemor Gro. 14	55 K15	Brown St. N. 7	43 J8	Canning Pl. 1	44 M8
Bird Av. 14	56 M14	Braemor Pk. 14	55 K14	Brown St. S. 8	42 H10	Cannon Rock Vw.,	31 BB3
Bishop St. 8	43 K10	Braemor Rd. 14	55 K15	Brunswick Pl. 2	44 M9	Howth	
Black Pitts 8	43 J10	Brainborough Ter. 8	42 H10	*Pearse St.*		Canon Lillis Av. 1	44 M8
Black St. 7	42 G8	*South Circular Rd.*		Brunswick St. N. 7	43 J8	Canon Mooney	45 N9
Blackberry La. 6	49 K11	Braithwaite St. 8	42 H9	Brusna Cotts., D.L.	59 R15	Gdns. 4	
Blackhall Par. 7	43 J8	Brakens La. 2	44 L8	Buckingham St.	36 L7	*Cambridge Rd.*	
Blackhall Pl. 7	42 H8	*Moss St.*		Lwr. 1		Capel St. 1	43 K8
Blackhall St. 7	43 J8	Branch Rd. N. 1	62 P8	Buckingham St.	36 L7	Cappagh Av. 11	21 F2
Blackheath Av. 3	38 Q6	Branch Rd. S. 1	62 P8	Upper 1		Cappagh Dr. 11	21 F3
Blackheath Dr. 3	38 P6	Brandon Rd. 12	47 E11	Bulfin Gdns. 8	41 F9	Cappagh Rd. 11	21 E2
Blackheath Gdns. 3	38 P6	Breakwater Rd. S. 1	62 P8	Bulfin Rd. 8	41 F10	Captains Av. 12	47 F12
Blackheath Gro. 3	38 P6	Bregia Rd. 7	34 H6	Bulfin St. 8	41 F9	Captains Dr. 12	47 F12
Blackheath Pk. 3	38 P6	Brehan Rd. 4	45 O9	Bull All. St. 8	43 J9	Captains Rd. 12	47 F12
Blackhorse Av. 7	32 D5	Brendan Behan Ct. 1	36 L7	Bunratty Av. 5	26 P2	Caragh Rd. 7	34 G7
Blackhorse Bri. 8	41 E10	*Russell St.*		Bunratty Dr. 5	26 P2	Carberry Rd. 9	36 M5
Blackhorse Gro. 7	34 H7	Brendan Dr.		Bunratty Rd. 5	25 O2	Cardiff Bri. 7	35 J7
Blackrock Coll., D.L.	58 Q14	(Ceide Brendain) 5	26 P3	Bunting Rd. 12	46 D12	*Phibsborough Rd.*	
Blackrock Sta., D.L.	59 R14	Brendan Rd. 4	50 M12	Burdett Av., D.L.	61 W17	Cardiff Castle Rd. 11	21 F3
Blackwater Rd. 11	34 H5	Brian Av. 3	36 M5	Burgess La. 7	43 J8	Cardiffs La. 2	44 M9
Blarney Pk. 12	48 G12	Brian Boru Av. 3	38 Q7	*Haymarket*		Cardiffsbridge Av. 11	21 F3
Blessington Ct. 7	35 K7	Brian Boru St. 3	38 Q7	Burgh Quay 2	43 K8	Cardiffsbridge Gro. 11	21 F2
Blessington St.		Brian Rd. 3	36 M6	Burke Pl. 8	42 G9	*Cappagh Rd.*	
Blessington St. 7	35 K7	Brian Ter. 3	36 M6	Burleigh Ct. 4	50 L11	Cardiffsbridge Rd. 11	21 F3
Bloom Cotts. 8	43 J10	Briarfield Gro. 5	28 T3	Burlington Gdns. 4	44 L10	Cards La. 2	44 L9
Bloomfield Av.	50 L11	Briarfield Rd. 5	27 S3	Burlington Rd. 4	44 L10	*Townsend St.*	
(Donnybrook) 4		Briarfield Vills. 5	28 T3	Burris Ct. 8	43 J9	Carleton Rd. 3	37 N6
Bloomfield Av.	43 J10	Brickfield Dr. 12	42 G10	*School Ho. La. W.*		Carlingford Par. 2	44 M9
(Portobello) 8		Brickfield La. 8	42 H10	Burrow Rd., Howth	30 X2	Carlingford Rd. 9	35 K6
Bloomfield Pk. 8	49 J11	Bride Rd. 8	43 J9	Burrowfield Rd.,	29 W2	Carlisle Av. 4	50 M12
Bluebell Av. 12	46 D11	Bride St. 8	43 J9	Baldoyle		Carlisle St. 8	43 J10
Bluebell Rd. 12	46 D11	Bride St. New 8	43 K10	Bushfield Av. 4	50 M12	Carlton Ct. 3	37 O6
Blythe Av. 3	44 M8	Bridge St. 4	45 N9	Bushfield Pl. 4	50 L12	Carmans Hall 8	43 J9
Church Rd.		Bridge St. Lwr. 8	43 J9	Bushfield Ter. 4	50 L12	Carndonagh Dr. 5	28 T2
Boden Wd. 14	54 H16	Bridge St. Upper 8	43 J9	Bushy Pk. Gdns. 6	55 J14	Carndonagh Lawn 5	28 T2
Bolton St. 1	43 K8	Bridgefoot St. 8	43 J9	Bushy Pk. Rd. 6	54 H14	Carndonagh Pk. 5	28 T2
Bon Secours Hosp. 9	23 K4	Brighton Av. 3	37 N6	Butterfield Av. 14	53 F16	Carndonagh Rd. 5	28 T2
Bond Dr. 1	45 O8	Brighton Av. 6	49 J13	Butterfield Clo. 14	54 G16	Carnew St. 7	34 H7
Bond Rd. 3	45 N8	Brighton Av., D.L.	60 T16	Butterfield Cres. 14	54 H15	Carnlough Rd. 7	34 G5
Bond St. 8	42 H9	Brighton Gdns. 6	49 J13	Butterfield Dr. 14	54 H16	Caroline Row 4	45 N9
Bonham St. 8	42 H9	Brighton Rd. 6	49 J13	Butterfield Gro. 14	54 G15	*Bridge St.*	
Boolavogue Rd. 3	36 M7	Brighton Sq. 6	49 J13	Butterfield Orchard 14	54 H16	Carraroe Av. 5	27 S2
Booterstown Av., D.L.	58 P15	Brighton Vale, D.L.	59 S15	Butterfield Pk. 14	54 G16	Carrick Brennan	60 T16
Booterstown Pk., D.L.	58 P15	Britain Pl. 1	43 K8	Byrnes La. 1	43 K8	Lawn, D.L.	
Botanic Av. 9	35 K5	Britain Quay 2	45 N9			Carrick Ter. 8	42 H10
Botanic Gdns. 11	35 J5	Broadstone 7	35 J7	Cabra Dr. 7	34 H6	Carrickbrack Heath,	30 Y3
Botanic Pk. 9	35 K5	Broadstone Av. 7	35 J7	Cabra Gro. 7	34 H6	Howth	
Botanic Rd. 9	35 J6	*Phibsborough Rd.*		Cabra Pk. 7	35 J6	Carrickbrack Hill,	30 Y3
Botanic Vills. 9	35 K5	Brook Ct., D.L.	60 T16	Cabra Rd. 7	34 G6	Howth	
Botanic Rd.		Brookfield 5	26 Q3	Cadogan Rd. 3	36 M6	Carrickbrack Lawn,	30 Y4
Bothar Ainninn	26 Q3	Brookfield 6	50 L13	Calderwood Av. 9	24 M4	Howth	
(Ennel Rd.) 5		Brookfield, D.L.	58 Q15	Calderwood Clo. 9	36 M5	Carrickbrack Rd.,	30 Y4
Bothar Aird An	21 F4	Brookfield Av., D.L.	59 R15	Calderwood Gro. 9	36 M5	Howth	
Tobair 11		Brookfield Est. 12	48 G13	Calderwood Rd. 9	36 M5	Carrickbrennan Rd.,	60 T16
(Springmount Rd.)		Brookfield Pl., D.L.	59 R15	Caledon Rd. 3	36 M7	D.L.	
Bothar An Easa	27 R4	Brookfield Rd. 8	42 G9	Callary Rd.,	57 O15	Carrickmount Av. 14	55 K16
(Watermill Rd.) 5		Brookfield St. 8	42 G9	Stillorgan		Carrickmount Dr. 14	55 K16
Bothar Chille Na	46 D12	Brooklands 4	51 O12	Camac Pk. 12	46 C11	Carrickmount Pk. 14	55 K16
Manac 12		Brooklawn 3	37 O6	Camac Ter. 8	42 G9	Carrigallen Dr. 11	22 G4
(Walkinstown Rd.)		Brooklawn, D.L.	58 Q15	*Bow Bri.*		*Carrigallen Rd.*	
Bothar Colbeard	41 E9	Brooklawn Av., D.L.	59 S16	Cambells Ct. 7	43 J8	Carrigallen Pk. 11	22 G4
(Con Colbert Rd.) 8		Brookmount Av.,	52 D16	*Little Britain St.*		*Carrigallen Rd.*	
Bothar Dhroichead	21 F3	Tallaght		Cambridge Av. 4	45 O9	Carrigallen Rd. 11	22 G4
Chiarduibh 11		Brookmount Lawn 4	52 D16	Cambridge La. 6	49 K12	Carrow Rd. 12	41 E10
(Cardiffsbridge Rd.)		*Tallaght Rd.*		Cambridge Rd. 4	45 N9	Carysfort Av., D.L.	59 R16
Bothar Phairc An	33 F6	Brookvale Downs 14	54 H14	Cambridge Rd.	49 K12	Casana Vw.,	31 BB4
Bhailtini 7		Brookvale Rd. 4	50 M12	(Rathmines) 6		Howth	
(Villa Pk. Rd.)		Brookville 11	22 G2	Cambridge St. 4	45 N9	Casement Dr. 11	21 F2
Bothar Raitleann 12	48 G13	Brookville Cres. 5	26 P2	Cambridge Ter. 6	50 L11	Casement Grn. 11	21 F2
(Rathland Rd.)		Brookville Pk. 5	26 Q2	Cambridge Vills. 6	49 K12	Casement Gro. 11	21 F2
Boundary Rd. 1	37 O7	Brookville Pk., D.L.	60 S17	*Belgrave St.*		Casement Pk. 11	21 F2
Bow Bri. 8	42 G9	Brookwood Av. 5	26 P4	Camden Lock 4	45 N9	Casement Pk.,	60 T17
Bow La. E. 2	43 K9			*South Docks Rd.*		D.L.	

Name	Map	Grid
Connolly Sta. 1	44	L8
Conor Clune Rd. 7	33	L6
Conquer Hill Rd. 3	38	Q7
Conquer Hill Ter. 3	38	Q6
Constitution Hill 7	43	J8
Convent Av. 3	36	M6
Convent La. 14	54	H16
Convent Rd., D.L.	61	U16
Convent Rd.	59	R15
(Blackrock), D.L.		
Convent Vw. Cotts. 7	33	F5
Conway Ct. 2	44	M9
Macken St.		
Conyngham Rd. 8	41	F8
Cook St. 8	43	J9
Coolamber Pk. 14	53	F16
Coolatree Pk. 9	24	M3
Coolatree Rd. 9	25	N3
Cooleen Av. 9	24	M2
Coolevin La. 8	43	J10
Long La.		
Cooley Rd. 12	41	E10
Coolgariff Rd. 9	24	M3
Coolgreena Clo. 9	25	N3
Coolgreena Rd. 9	25	N3
Coolock Av. 5	26	P2
Coolock Clo. 5	26	P2
Coolock Ct. 5	26	P2
Coolock Dr. 5	26	P2
Coolock Grn. 5	26	P2
Coolock Gro. 5	26	P3
Coolock Village 5	26	P3
Coolrua Dr. 9	24	M3
Coombe, The 8	43	J9
Cope St. 2	43	K9
Copeland Av. 3	37	N6
Copeland Gro. 3	37	N6
Copper All. 8	43	K9
Coppinger Clo., D.L.	58	Q16
Coppinger Glade, D.L.	58	Q16
Coppinger Wk., D.L.	58	Q16
Coppinger Wd., D.L.	58	Q16
Coppingers Row 2	43	K9
William St. S.		
Corballis Row 8	43	J10
Kevin St. Upper		
Cork Hill 2	43	K9
Cork St. 8	42	H10
Cormack Ter. 6	54	H14
Corn Ex. Pl. 2	44	L8
George's Quay		
Cornmarket 8	43	J9
Corporation Bldgs. 8	42	G9
Corporation Pl. 1	44	L8
Corporation St. 1	44	L8
Corrib Rd. 6	48	G13
Corrig Av., D.L.	61	V17
Corrig Castle Ter.,D.L.	61	V16
Corrig Clo. 12	52	C14
Lugnaquilla Av.		
Corrig Pk., D.L.	61	V17
Corrig Rd., D.L.	61	V17
Corrybeg 12	53	F16
Cottage Pl. 1	35	K6
Portland Pl.		
Coulson Av. 6	49	J13
Coultry Way 9	24	L2
Court, The 3	37	O6
Clontarf Rd.		
Court, The 5	27	S4
Courts of Justice 7	43	J8
Cow Parlour 8	43	J10
Cowbooter La.,	31	BB3
Howth		
Cowley Pl. 7	35	K6
Cowper Downs 6	49	K13
Cowper Dr. 6	50	L13
Cowper Gdns. 6	50	L13
Cowper Rd. 6	49	K13
Cowper St. 7	34	H7
Cowper Village 6	49	K13
Craigford Av. 5	25	O4
Craigford Dr. 5	25	O4
Craigmore Gdns.,	59	S15
D.L.		
Crampton Bldgs. 2	43	K9
Temple Bar		
Crampton Ct. 2	43	K9
Crampton Quay 2	43	K8
Crane La. 2	43	K9
Crane St. 8	42	H9
Cranfield Pl. 4	45	O10
Cranford Ct. 4	51	O13
Cranmer La. 4	44	M10
Crannagh 6	50	M13
Crannagh Gro. 14	55	J14
Crannagh Pk. 14	55	J15
Crannagh Rd. 14	54	H15
Crawford Av. 9	35	K6
Creighton St. 2	44	L9
Cremona Rd. 10	40	C9
Cremore Av. 11	23	J4
Cremore Cres. 11	23	J4
Cremore Dr. 11	23	J4
Cremore Heights 11	23	J3
Ballygall Rd. E.		
Cremore Lawn 11	23	J4
Cremore Pk. 11	23	J4
Cremore Rd. 11	23	J4
Cremorne 14	53	F16
Crescent, The	50	M12
(Donnybrook) 4		
Crescent, The 9	24	M4
Crescent Gdns. 3	36	M7
Crescent Pl. 3	37	N6
Crescent Vills. 9	35	K6
Crestfield Av. 9	24	L3
Crestfield Clo. 9	24	L3
Crestfield Dr. 9	24	L3
Crestfield Pk. 9	24	L3
Crestfield Clo.		
Croaghpatrick Rd. 7	33	F6
Crofton Av., D.L.	60	U16
Crofton Rd., D.L.	60	U15
Crofton Ter., D.L.	60	U15
Croker La. 8	42	H9
Cromcastle Av. 5	25	O2
Cromcastle Dr. 5	25	O2
Cromcastle Grn. 5	25	O2
Cromcastle Pk. 5	25	O2
Cromcastle Rd. 5	25	O2
Cromwells Fort Rd. 12	46	D12
Cromwells	42	G9
Quarters 8		
Cross & Passion	56	M14
Coll. 9		
Cross Av., Blackrock	58	P14
Cross Av., D.L.	60	U16
Cross Guns Bri. 7	35	J6
Cross Kevin St. 8	43	K10
Crosthwaite Pk. E.,	61	V17
D.L.		
Crosthwaite Pk. S.,	61	V17
D.L.		
Crosthwaite Pk. W.,	61	V17
D.L.		
Crosthwaite Ter., D.L.	61	V16
Crotty Av. 12	47	E12
Crow St. 2	43	K9
Crown All. 2	43	K9
Temple Bar		
Croydon Gdns. 3	36	M5
Croydon Grn. 3	36	M6
Croydon Pk. Av. 3	36	M5
Croydon Ter. 3	36	M5
Crumlin Rd. 12	47	F11
Cuala Rd. 7	34	H6
Cuckoo La. 7	43	J8
Cuffe La. 2	43	K10
Cuffe St. 2	43	K10
Cullenswood Gdns. 6	50	L12
Cullenswood Pk. 6	50	L12
Cumberland Rd. 2	44	L10
Cumberland St., D.L.	60	U16
Cumberland St. N. 1	35	K7
Cumberland St. S. 2	44	L9
Curlew Rd. 12	47	E11
Curzon St. 8	43	K10
Custom Ho. 1	44	L8
Custom Ho. Quay 1	44	L8
Cymric Rd. 4	45	O9
Cypress Downs 6	53	F15
Cypress Dr. 6	53	F16
Cypress Garth 6	53	F15
Cypress Gro. N. 6	53	F15
Cypress Gro. Rd. 6	53	F15
Cypress Gro. S. 6	53	F15
Cypress Lawn 6	53	F15
Cypress Pk. 6	53	F15
Cypress Rd.,	57	O15
Stillorgan		
Dale Clo., Stillorgan	57	O16
Dale Dr., Stillorgan	57	O16
Dame Ct. 2	43	K9
Dame La. 2	43	K9
Dame St. 2	43	K9
Danesfort 3	37	O6
Daneswell Rd. 9	35	K5
Dangan Av. 12	47	F13
Dangan Dr. 12	47	F13
Dangan Pk. 12	47	F13
Daniel St. 8	43	J10
Danieli Dr. 5	26	P4
Danieli Rd. 5	26	P4
Dargle Rd. 9	35	K6
Darley St. 6	49	J11
Darleys Ter. 8	42	H10
Darling Est. 7	33	E5
Dartmouth La. 6	50	L11
Dartmouth Pl. 6	49	K11
Dartmouth Rd. 6	49	K11
Dartmouth Sq. 6	50	L11
Dartmouth Ter. 6	49	K11
Dartry Cotts. 6	55	K14
Dartry Pk. 6	49	K13
Dartry Rd. 6	49	K13
David Pk. 9	35	K6
David Rd. 9	35	K6
Davis Pl. 8	43	J9
Thomas Davis St. S.		
Davitt Rd. 12	41	F10
Dawson Ct. 2	43	K9
Stephen St.		
Dawson Ct., D.L.	58	Q15
Dawson La. 2	44	L9
Dawson St. 2	43	K9
De Burgh Rd. 7	42	H8
De Courcy Sq. 9	35	J5
De Vesci Ter., D.L.	60	U16
Deaf & Dumb	34	G6
Institution 7		
Dean St. 8	43	J10
Dean Swift Grn. 11	23	K3
Dean Swift Rd. 11	23	J3
Swifts All.		
Deans Gra. Cem.,D.L.	60	S17
Deans Gra. Rd.,	59	S16
Stillorgan		
Deanstown Av. 11	21	F3
Deanstown Dr. 11	21	F3
Deanstown Grn.		
Deanstown Grn. 11	21	F3
Deanstown Pk. 11	21	F3
Deanstown Rd. 11	21	F3
Decies Rd. 10	40	C9
Deerpark Av.,	32	C5
Castleknock		
Deerpark Clo.,	32	C5
Castleknock		
Deerpark Dr.,	32	C5
Castleknock		
Deerpark Lawn,	32	C5
Castleknock		
Deerpark Rd.,	32	C5
Castleknock		
Deerpark Rd.,	57	O15
Stillorgan		
Del Val Av.,Kilbarrack	28	U3
Delville Rd. 11	23	J3
Delvin Rd. 7	34	H6
Demesne 5	38	P5
Denmark St. Great 1	35	K7
Denzille La. 2	44	L9
Denzille Pl. 2	44	L9
Denzille La.		
Department of	42	G8
Defence 7		
Infirmary Rd.		
Department of	35	K5
Defence 9		
St. Mobhi Rd.		
Dermot O'Hurley	45	N9
Av. 4		
Derravaragh Rd. 6	48	G13
Derry Dr. 12	47	F12
Derry Pk. 12	47	F12
Derry Rd. 12	47	F12
Derrynane Gdns. 4	45	N10
Derrynane Par. 7	35	K7
Desmond Av., D.L.	60	U16
Desmond St. 8	43	J10
Devenish Rd. 12	48	G12
Deverell Pl. 1	44	L8
Deverys La. 7	35	J6
Devoy Rd. 8	41	F10
Digges La. 2	43	K9
Stephen St.		
Digges St. 2	43	K10
Digges St. Lwr. 2	43	K10
Cuffe La.		
Dingle Rd. 7	34	G6
Dispensary La. 14	55	J16
Distillery Rd. 3	36	L6
Dock Pl. S. 4	44	M9
Dock St. S.		
Dock St. S. 4	44	M9
Dodder Dale 14	54	H15
Dodder Pk. Dr. 14	55	J14
Dodder Pk. Gro. 14	55	J14
Dodder Pk. Rd. 14	55	J14
Dodder Ter. 4	45	N9
Doddervale 6	55	K14
D'Olier St. 2	43	K8
Dollymount Av. 3	39	R6
Dollymount Gro. 3	39	R6
Dollymount Pk. 3	39	R6
Dollymount Ri. 3	39	R6
Dolphin Av. 8	42	H10
Dolphin Mkt. 8	42	H10
Dolphin's Barn St.		
Dolphin Rd. 12	42	G10
Dolphin's Barn 8	42	H10
Dolphin's Barn St. 8	42	H10
Dominican Convent 7	33	F5
Dominick La. 1	43	K8
Dominick Pl. 1	43	K8
Dominick St., D.L.	60	U16
Dominick St. Lwr. 1	43	K8
Dominick St.	35	J7
Upper 7		
Domville Dr. 12	53	F15
Domville Rd. 12	53	F15
Donaghmede Av. 5	28	T2
Donaghmede Dr. 5	28	T2
Donaghmede Pk. 5	28	T2
Donaghmede Rd. 5	27	S2
Donard Rd. 12	47	E11
Donelan Av. 8	42	G9
Donnybrook Grn. 4	51	N13
Donnybrook Manor 4	50	M12
Donnybrook Rd. 4	50	M12
Donnycarney Rd. 9	37	N5
Donore Av. 8	42	H10
Donore Rd. 8	42	H10
Donore Ter. 8	42	H10
Brown St. S.		
Donovans La. 8	43	J10
Clanbrassil St. Lwr.		
Doon Av. 7	34	H7
Doris St. 4	45	N9
Dornden Pk.,	63	P13
Booterstown		
Dorset La. 1	35	K7
Dorset Pl. 1	35	K7
Dorset St. Lwr.		
Dorset St. Lwr. 1	35	K7
Dorset St. Upper 1	35	K7
Dowker's La. 8	43	J10

Name	No.	Grid
Dowland Rd. 12	47	E12
Dowling's Ct. 2	44	L9
Lombard St. E.		
Dowling's Ct. S. 2	44	L9
Lombard St. E.		
Downpatrick Rd. 12	48	G11
Dowth Av. 7	34	H6
Drapier Grn. 11	23	J3
Drapier Rd. 11	23	J3
Drimnagh Castle 12	46	D11
Drimnagh Rd. 12	47	E11
Dromard Rd. 12	47	E11
Dromawling Rd. 9	25	N3
Drombawn Av. 9	25	N3
Dromeen Av. 9	25	N3
Dromlee Cres. 9	25	N3
Drommartin Castle 14	56	M16
Dromnanane Pk. 9	25	N3
Dromnanane Rd. 9	25	N3
Dromore Rd. 12	47	F11
Drumalee Av. 7	34	H7
Drumalee Rd.		
Drumalee Ct. 7	34	H7
Drumalee Rd.		
Drumalee Dr. 7	34	H7
Drumalee Rd.		
Drumalee Gro. 7	34	H7
Drumalee Rd.		
Drumalee Pk. 7	34	H7
Drumalee Rd. 7	34	H7
Drumcliffe Dr. 7	34	G6
Drumcliffe Rd. 7	34	G6
Drumcondra Hosp. 3	35	K6
Drumcondra Pk. 3	36	L6
Drumcondra Rd. Lwr. 9	35	K6
Drumcondra Rd. Upper 9	36	L5
Drummartin Clo. 4	57	N16
Drummartin Cres. 14	57	N16
Drummartin Rd. 14	57	N16
Drummartin Ter. 14	57	N16
Drummond Pl. 6	49	J11
Mount Drummond Av.		
Drury St. 2	43	K9
Dublin Corporation Food Mkt. 7	43	J8
St. Michan's St.		
Dublin Health Authority 8	42	H9
Dublin Rd., Howth	30	X2
Dublin Rd., Kilbarrack	29	V3
Dublin St., Baldoyle	29	V2
Dufferin Av. 8	43	J10
Duggan Pl. 6	49	K12
Rathmines Rd. Upper		
Duke La. 2	43	K9
Duke La. Lwr. 2	43	K9
Duke St.		
Duke Row 1	36	L7
North Circular Rd.		
Duke St. 2	43	K9
Dunamase, D.L.	58	Q14
Dunard Av. 7	34	G6
Dunard Ct. 7	34	G7
Dunard Dr. 7	34	G7
Dunard Pk. 7	34	G7
Dunard Rd. 7	34	G7
Dunard Wk. 7	34	G7
Dunbo Ter., Howth	31	AA2
Church St.		
Dundaniel Rd. 5	25	N2
Dundela Av., D.L.	61	W17
Dundela Haven, D.L.	61	W17
Dundrum Rd. 14	56	L16
Dunedin Ter., D.L.	60	T17
Dungar Ter., D.L.	61	V16
Northumberland Av.		
Dungriffan Rd., Howth	31	BB3
Dunleary Hill, D.L.	60	U16
Dunleary Rd., D.L.	60	U15
Dunluce Rd. 3	38	P5
Dunmanus Rd. 7	34	G6
Dunne St. 1	36	L7
Dunree Pk. 5	26	Q2
Dunseverick Rd. 3	38	P5
Dunsink Av. 11	21	F3
Dunsink Dr. 11	21	F3
Dunsink Gdns. 11	22	G3
Dunsink Grn. 1	22	G3
Dunsink Observatory, Castleknock	20	D3
Dunsink Pk. 11	21	F3
Dunsink Rd. 11	22	G3
Dunville Av. 6	50	L12
Dunville Ter. 6	49	K11
Mountpleasant Av. Upper		
Durham Rd. 4	51	O11
Durrow Rd. 12	48	G12
Eagle Hill Av. 6	48	H13
Earl Pl. 1	43	K8
Earl St. N. 1	43	K8
Earl St. S. 8	43	J9
Earls Ct. 7	34	G7
Earlsfort Mans. 2	43	K10
Adelaide Rd.		
Earlsfort Ter. 2	43	K10
East Oil Jetty 1	62	P9
East Rd. 3	44	M8
East Wall Rd. 3	36	M7
Eastern Breakwater 1	62	P9
Eastmoreland La. 4	44	M10
Eastmoreland Pl. 4	44	M10
Eaton Brae 14	55	K14
Eaton Pl., D.L.	59	S15
Eaton Rd. 6	48	H13
Eaton Sq. 6	48	H13
Eaton Sq., D.L.	59	S15
Ebenezer Ter. 8	42	H10
Eblana Av., D.L.	61	V16
Eblana Vills. 2	44	M9
Grand Canal St. Lwr.		
Eccles Ct. 1	36	L7
Eccles Pl.		
Eccles Pl. 7	35	K7
Eccles St. 7	35	K7
Echlin St. 8	42	H9
Eden Pk., D.L.	61	V17
Eden Pk. Dr. 14	57	N16
Eden Pk. Rd. 14	57	N16
Eden Quay 1	43	K8
Eden Rd. Lwr., D.L.	61	V17
Eden Rd. Upper, D.L.	61	V17
Eden Ter., D.L.	61	V17
Eden Vills., D.L.	61	V17
Edenbrook Dr. 14	54	G16
Edenbrook Pk. 14	54	G16
Edenmore Av. 5	26	Q3
Edenmore Cres. 5	27	R3
Edenmore Dr. 5	27	R3
Edenmore Gdns. 5	27	R3
Edenmore Grn. 5	27	R3
Edenmore Gro. 5	27	R3
Edenmore Pk. 5	26	Q3
Edenvale Rd. 6	50	L12
Effra Rd. 6	49	J12
Eglinton Ct. 4	50	M12
Eglinton Pk. 4	50	M12
Eglinton Pk., D.L.	61	V16
Eglinton Rd. 4	50	M12
Eglinton Sq. 4	50	M12
Eglinton Ter. 4	56	M16
Eglinton Ter. 14	56	M16
Eldon Ter. 8	43	J10
South Circular Rd.		
Elgin Rd. 4	50	M11
Elizabeth St. 3	36	L6
Elkwood 14	54	G16
Ellenfield Rd. 9	24	M3
Ellesmere Av. 7	34	H7
Ellis Quay 7	42	H8
Elliss St. 7	42	H8
Benburb St.		
Elm Gro., D.L.	59	R16
Elm Gro. Cotts. 7	33	E6
Blackhorse Av.		
Elm Mt. Av. 9	25	N4
Elm Mt. Clo. 9	25	N4
Elm Mt. Ct. 9	25	O4
Elm Mt. Cres. 5	25	N3
Elm Mt. Dr. 9	25	N4
Elm Mt. Gro. 9	25	N3
Elm Mt. Heights 9	25	N3
Elm Mt. Lawn 9	25	N3
Elm Mt. Pk. 9	25	N4
Elm Mt. Ri. 9	25	N4
Elm Mt. Rd. 5	25	N4
Elm Mt. Rd. 9	25	N4
Elm Mt. Vw. 9	25	N4
Elm Rd. 9	25	N4
Elmpark Av. 6	50	L11
Elmpark Ter. 6	48	H13
Elmpark Ter. (Ranelagh) 6	50	L11
Elms, The 4	51	O13
Elms, The, D.L.	58	Q15
Elmwood Av. 6	50	L11
Elmwood Av. Upper 6	50	L11
Elton Ct. 5	27	R2
Elton Dr.		
Elton Dr. 5	27	R2
Elton Pk. 5	27	R2
Elton Pk., D.L.	61	W17
Elton Wk. 5	27	R2
Elton Dr.		
Ely Pl. 2	44	L10
Ely Pl. Upper 2	44	L10
Embassy Lawn 14	56	M14
Emerald Cotts. 4	44	M10
Emerald Pl. 1	44	M8
Sheriff St. Lwr.		
Emerald Sq. 8	42	H10
Emerald St. 1	44	M8
Emily Pl. 1	44	L8
Sheriff St. Lwr.		
Emmet Ct. 8	41	E10
Emmet Rd. 8	41	F9
Emmet Sq., D.L.	58	Q14
Emmet St. 1	36	L7
Emmet St. (Haroldscross) 6	49	J11
Emor St. 8	43	J10
Emorville Av. 8	43	J10
Emorville Sq. 8	43	J10
South Circular Rd.		
Empress Pl. 1	36	L7
Enaville Rd. 3	36	M7
Engine All. 8	43	J9
Ennafort Av. (Ascal Dun Eanna) 5	26	Q4
Ennafort Ct. (Ceide Dun Eanna) 5	26	Q4
Ennafort Gro. 5	26	Q4
Ennafort Pk. 5	26	Q4
Ennafort Rd. 5	26	Q4
Ennel Av. 5	26	Q3
Ennel Dr. 5	26	Q3
Ennel Pk. 5	26	Q3
Enniskerry Rd. 7	35	J6
Erne Pl. 2	44	M9
Erne Pl. Little 2	44	M9
Erne St. Lwr. 2	44	M9
Erne St. Upper 2	44	M9
Erne Ter. Front 2	44	M9
Erne St. Upper		
Erne Ter. Rere 2	44	M9
Erne St. Upper		
Errigal Gdns. 12	47	E11
Errigal Rd. 12	47	E11
Erris Rd. 7	34	H6
Esmond Av. 3	36	M6
Esposito Rd. 12	47	E12
Essex Quay 8	43	K9
Essex St. E. 2	43	K9
Essex St. W. 8	43	K9
Estate Av. 4	63	P13
Estate Cotts. 4	44	M10
Northumberland Rd.		
Eugene St. 8	42	H10
Eustace St. 2	43	K9
Everton Av. 7	34	H7
Evora Pk., Howth	31	AA2
Evora Ter., Howth	31	AA2
St. Lawrence Rd.		
Ewington La. 8	42	H9
Exchange Ct. 2	43	K9
Dame St.		
Exchange St. Lwr. 8	43	K9
Exchange St. Upper 8	43	K9
Cork Hill		
Exchequer St. 2	43	K9
Faber Ct., D.L.	60	T17
Fade St. 2	43	K9
Fairbrook Lawn 14	54	H16
Fairfield Av. 3	36	M7
Fairfield Pk. 6	49	J13
Fairfield Rd. (Glasnevin) 9	35	K5
Fairlawn Pk. 11	22	G4
Fairlawn Rd.		
Fairlawn Rd. 11	22	G4
Fairview 3	36	M6
Fairview Av. (Irishtown) 4	45	N9
Fairview Av. Lwr. 3	36	M6
Fairview Av. Upper 3	36	M6
Fairview Grn. 3	36	M6
Fairview Pas. 3	36	M6
Fairview Strand		
Fairview Strand 3	36	M6
Fairview Ter. 3	36	M6
Fairways 14	54	G15
Fairways Av. 11	22	H3
Fairways Grn. 11	22	H3
Fairways Pk. 11	22	H3
Falcarragh Rd. 9	24	L3
Farmhill Dr. 14	56	M15
Farmhill Pk. 14	56	M16
Farmhill Rd. 14	56	M15
Farney Pk. 4	45	O10
Farnham Cres. 11	22	G3
Farnham Dr. 11	22	G3
Farrenboley Cotts. 14	56	L14
Farrenboley Pk. 14	56	L14
Father Matthew Bri. 7	43	J9
Fatima Mans. 8	42	G10
Faughart Rd. 12	48	G12
Faussagh Av. 7	34	G6
Faussagh Rd. 7	34	H6
Fenian St. 2	44	L9
Fergus Rd. 6	54	H14
Ferguson Rd. 9	35	K5
Ferndale Av. 11	22	H3
Ferndale Rd. 11	22	H3
Fernhill Av. 12	53	E14
Fernhill Pk. 12	53	E14
Fernhill Rd. 12	53	E14
Ferns Rd. 12	48	G12
Fernvale Dr. 12	47	F11
Ferrard Rd. 6	49	J13
Fertullagh Rd. 7	34	H6
Field Av. 12	47	E12
Fields Ter. 6	50	L11
Ranelagh Rd.		
Fifth Av. 8	42	G10
Findlater Pl. 1	43	K8
Findlater St., D.L.	61	V17
Findlaters St. 7	42	G8
Fingal Av. (Clontarf) 3	38	Q6
Fingal Pl. 7	34	H7
Fingal St. 8	42	H10
Finglas Bri. 11	22	H4
Finglas Pk. 11	22	H2
Finglas Pl. 11	22	G3
Finglas Rd. 11	22	G3
Finglas Rd. Old 11	23	J4
Finsbury Pk. 14	56	L16
First Av. 1	44	M8
First Av. (Inchicore) 10	40	D9
Fishamble St. 8	43	J9
Fitzgerald Pk., D.L.	60	U17
Fitzgerald St. 6	49	J11
Fitzgibbon La. 1	36	L7
Fitzgibbon St. 1	36	L7

Name	Pg	Grid
Fitzmaurice Rd. 11	23	J3
Fitzroy Av. 3	36	L6
Fitzwilliam Ct. 2	44	L10
Pembroke St. Upper		
Fitzwilliam La. 2	44	L10
Fitzwilliam Pl. 2	44	L10
Fitzwilliam Quay 4	45	N9
Fitzwilliam Sq. E. 2	44	L10
Fitzwilliam Sq. N. 2	44	L10
Fitzwilliam Sq. S. 2	44	L10
Fitzwilliam Sq. W. 2	44	L10
Fitzwilliam St.	45	N9
(Ringsend) 4		
Fitzwilliam St. Lwr. 2	44	L10
Fitzwilliam St.	44	L10
Upper 2		
Fleet St. 2	43	K9
Fleming Rd. 9	35	K5
Flemings La. 4	44	M10
Haddington Rd.		
Flemings Pl. 4	44	L10
Fleurville, D.L.	59	R16
Floraville Rd.	50	M12
(Donnybrook) 4		
Florence St. 8	49	K11
Lennox St.		
Foley St. 1	44	L8
Fontenoy St. 7	35	J7
Fonthill Pk. 14	54	H16
Fonthill Rd. 14	54	H16
Forbes La. 8	42	H9
Forbes St. 2	44	M9
Fortfield Av. 6	54	G14
Fortfield Ct. 6	54	G14
Fortfield Dr. 6	54	G15
Fortfield Gdns. 6	49	K13
Fortfield Gro. 6	54	G14
Fortfield Pk. 6	54	G15
Fortfield Ter. 6	49	K13
Forth Rd. 3	37	N7
Fortview Av. 3	38	Q7
Foster Cotts. 7	35	J7
Phibsborough Rd.		
Foster Pl. S. 2	43	K9
Foster Ter. 3	36	L7
Fosterbrook, D.L.	58	P14
Fosters, The,	57	O15
Stillorgan		
Fosters Av., Stillorgan	57	O15
Fountain Pl. 7	43	J8
Fountain Rd. 8	42	G8
Fourth Av. 1	44	M8
Fourth Av. 8	42	G10
Fownes St. 2	43	K9
Foxfield Av. 5	27	S3
Foxfield Cres. 5	28	T3
Foxfield Dr. 5	28	T3
Foxfield Grn. 5	28	T3
Foxfield Gro. 5	27	S3
Foxfield Heights 5	27	S3
Foxfield Lawn 5	27	S3
Foxfield Pk. 5	28	T4
Foxfield Rd. 5	27	S3
Foxfield St. John 5	28	T3
Foxhill Av. 5	27	R2
Foxhill Clo. 5	27	R2
Foxhill Ct. 5	27	R2
Foxhill Cres. 5	27	R2
Foxhill Dr. 5	27	R2
Foxhill Grn. 5	27	R2
Foxhill Gro. 5	27	R2
Foxhill Lawn 5	27	R2
Foxhill Pk. 5	27	R2
Foxhill Way 5	27	R2
Foxs La. 5	28	T4
Foyle Rd. 3	36	M6
Francis St. 8	43	J9
Frankfort 14	56	L15
Frankfort Av. 6	49	K13
Frankfort Castle 14	56	L15
Frankfort Pk. 14	56	L15
Frascati Pk., D.L.	59	R15
Frascati Rd., D.L.	59	R15
Frederick Ct. N. 1	35	K7
Frederick La. 2	44	L9
Frederick La. N. 1	35	K7
Frederick St. N. 1	35	K7
Frederick St. S. 2	44	L9
Gardiner St. Lwr.		
Frenchmans La. 1	44	L8
Gardiner St. Lwr.		
Friarsland Av. 14	56	M15
Friarsland Rd. 14	56	M15
Friary Av. 7	43	J8
Fumballys La. 8	43	J10
Furry Pk. 5	38	P5
Furry Pk. Rd. 5	38	Q5
Furze Rd.,	32	C7
Castleknock		
Gaelic St. 3	36	M7
Gairdini Sheinleasa 9	23	K2
Galmoy Rd. 7	34	H6
Galtymore Clo. 12	41	E10
Galtymore Dr. 12	41	F10
Galtymore Pk. 12	47	E11
Galtymore Rd. 12	47	E11
Garden La. 8	43	J9
Gardiner La. 1	36	L7
Gardiner Pl. 1	35	K7
Gardiner Row 1	35	K7
Gardiner St. Lwr. 1	36	L7
Gardiner St. Middle 1	36	L7
Gardiner St. Upper 1	35	K7
Gardiners Row, D.L.	58	P14
Gardini Lein	26	Q4
(Lein Gdns.) 5		
Gardini Phairc An	33	F6
Bhailtini		
(Villa Pk. Gdns.) 7		
Garriglea Gdns., D.L.	60	U17
Garryowen Rd. 10	40	C9
Gartan Av. 9	35	K6
Garville Av. 6	49	J13
Garville Av. Upper 6	49	J13
Garville Rd. 6	49	J13
Geoffrey Keating	43	J10
Rd. 8		
O'Curry Rd.		
George's Av., D.L.	59	R15
George's Hill 7	43	J8
George's La. 7	43	J8
George's Pl. 1	35	K7
George's Pl., D.L.	61	U16
George's Pl.	59	R15
(Blackrock), D.L.		
George's Quay 2	44	L8
George's St. Lwr.	60	U16
D.L.		
George's St.	61	V16
Upper, D.L.		
Gerald St. 4	44	M9
Geraldine St. 7	35	J7
Geraldine Ter. 6	50	L13
Gilbert Rd. 8	43	J10
Gilford Av. 4	51	O11
Gilford Ct. 4	51	O11
Gilford Dr. 4	51	O11
Gilford Pk. 4	51	O11
Gilford Rd. 4	51	O11
Glanarriff Rd.,	33	E5
Ashtown		
Glandore Pk., D.L.	60	U17
Glandore Rd. 9	36	M5
Glasanaon Ct. 11	22	H3
Glasanaon Pk.		
Glasanaon Pk. 11	22	H3
Glasanaon Rd. 11	22	H3
Glasaree Rd. 11	22	H3
Glasgow Ct. 14	56	L14
Glasilawn Av. 11	23	J4
Glasilawn Rd. 11	22	H4
Glasmeen Rd. 11	22	H4
Glasnamana Pl. 11	22	H4
Glasnamana Rd. 11	22	H4
Glasnevin Av. 11	22	H2
Glasnevin Bri. 9	35	K5
Glasnevin Ct. 11	22	H4
Glasnevin Dr. 11	23	J3
Glasnevin Hill 9	35	K5
Glasnevin Pk. 11	23	J2
Glasthule Bldgs., D.L.	61	W17
Glasthule Rd., D.L.	61	W17
Gleann Na Smol, D.L.	59	S16
Glebe Av. 11	22	G3
Gledswood Av. 14	56	M14
Gledswood Clo. 14	56	M14
Gledswood Pk. 14	56	M14
Glen, The, D.L.	61	V17
Glengara Clo.		
Glenaan Rd. 9	24	L3
Glenabbey Rd.,	57	O16
Stillorgan		
Glenageary Rd.	61	V17
Lwr., D.L.		
Glenageary Rd.	60	U17
Upper, D.L.		
Glenageary Wds.,	60	U17
D.L.		
Glenanne 12	48	G13
Glenard Av. 7	34	H7
Glenarm Av. 9	36	L6
Glenart Av., D.L.	58	Q16
Glenaulin Dr.	40	C8
(Ceide Glennaluinn),		
Chapelizod		
Glenavy Pk. 6	48	G13
Glenayle Rd. 5	27	R2
Glenayr Rd. 6	55	J14
Glenbeigh Pk. 7	34	G7
Glenbeigh Rd. 7	34	G7
Glenbower Pk. 14	56	L16
Glenbrook Pk. 14	54	H16
Glenbrook Rd. 7	33	E5
Glencar Rd. 7	34	G7
Glencarrig, Howth	30	Y2
Glencloy Rd. 9	24	L3
Glencorp Rd. 9	24	M3
Glendale Pk. 12	53	F14
Glendalough Rd. 9	35	K6
Glendhu Pk.,	33	E5
Ashtown		
Glendhu Rd.,	33	E5
Ashtown		
Glendoo Clo. 12	52	C14
Lugnaquilla Av.		
Glendown Av. 12	53	E14
Glendown Clo. 12	53	E14
Glendown Gro.		
Glendown Ct. 12	53	E14
Glendown Cres. 12	53	E14
Glendown Grn. 12	53	E14
Glendown Gro.		
Glendown Gro. 12	53	E14
Glendown Lawn 12	53	E14
Glendown Pk. 12	53	E14
Glendown Rd. 12	53	F14
Glendun Rd. 9	24	L3
Glenealy Rd. 12	48	H11
Glenfarne Rd. 5	26	Q2
Glengara Clo., D.L.	61	V17
Glengara Pk., D.L.	61	V17
Glengariff Pk. 7	35	K6
Glenhill Av. 11	22	H3
Glenhill Ct. 11	22	H3
Glenhill Dr. 11	22	H3
Glenhill Gro. 11	22	H3
Glenhill Rd. 11	22	H3
Glenhill Vills. 11	22	H3
Glenhill Pk.		
Glenmalure Pk. 8	42	G10
Glenmalure Sq. 6	50	L13
Glenmore Rd. 7	34	G7
Glenomena Gro.,	57	O14
Booterstown		
Glenomena Pk.,	51	O13
Booterstown		
Glenties Dr. 11	21	F4
Glenties Pk. 11	21	F4
Glentow Rd. 9	24	L3
Glentworth Pk. 5	27	R2
Sládemore Av.		
Glenview Lawns,	52	D16
Tallaght		
Glenview Pk.,	52	C16
Tallaght		
Glenwood Rd. 5	26	Q3
Gloucester La. 1	44	L8
Sean McDermott St. Lwr.		
Gloucester Pl. 1	36	L7
Gloucester Pl. Lwr. 1	44	L8
Gloucester Pl.	36	L7
Upper 1		
Gloucester St. S. 2	44	L8
Gloucester Ter. 1	36	L7
Glovers All. 2	43	K9
Goatstown Av. 14	56	M15
Goatstown Rd. 14	57	N15
Golden Bri. 8	41	E9
Golden La. 8	43	K9
Goldenbridge Av. 8	41	F10
Goldenbridge Gdns. 8	41	F10
Goldenbridge Ter. 8	41	E9
Connolly Av.		
Goldsmith St. 7	35	J7
Gordon Pl. 2	43	K10
Richmond St. S.		
Gordon St. 4	44	M9
Gorsefield Ct. 5	26	Q3
Gortbeg Av. 11	22	G4
Gortbeg Rd.		
Gortbeg Dr. 11	22	G4
Gortbeg Rd.		
Gortbeg Pk. 11	22	G4
Gortbeg Rd.		
Gortbeg Rd. 11	22	G4
Gortmore Av. 11	22	G4
Gortmore Dr. 11	22	G4
Gortmore Pk. 11	22	G4
Gortmore Rd.		
Gortmore Rd. 11	22	G4
Government	44	L9
Building 2		
Grace O'Malley Dr.,	31	AA3
Howth		
Grace O'Malley Rd.,	31	AA3
Howth		
Grace Pk. Av. 3	36	L6
Grace Pk. Ct. 9	24	M3
Grace Pk. Gdns. 9	36	L5
Grace Pk. Heights 9	24	M4
Grace Pk. Meadows 9	25	N4
Grace Pk. Rd. 9	36	L5
Grace Pk. Ter. 9	36	M5
Gracefield, D.L.	58	Q15
Gracefield Av. 5	26	Q4
Gracefield Rd. 5	26	P4
Grafton St. 2	43	K9
Graham Ct. 1	35	K7
Granby La. 1	35	K7
Granby Pl. 1	43	K8
Granby Row 1	35	K7
Grand Canal Bk.	49	K11
(Ranelagh) 6		
Grand Canal	42	H9
Harbour 8		
James's St.		
Grand Canal Pl. N. 8	42	H9
Grand Canal Quay 2	44	M9
Grand Canal St.	44	M9
Lwr. 2		
Grand Canal St.	44	M10
Upper 4		
Grand Canal Vw. 8	42	G10
Grand Par. 6	49	K11
Grange Downs 14	55	J16
Grange Gro., D.L.	60	S17
Grange Pk. 14	54	H16
Grange Pk. Av. 5	27	S3
Grange Pk. Clo. 5	27	S3
Grange Pk. Cres. 5	27	S3
Grange Pk. Dr. 5	27	S3
Grange Pk. Grn. 5	27	S3
Grange Pk. Gro. 5	27	S3
Grange Pk. Par. 5	27	S3
Grange Pk. Ri. 5	27	S3
Grange Pk. Rd. 5	27	S3
Grange Pk. Wk. 5	27	S3
Grange Rd. 5	27	S2
Grange Rd.	27	R4
(Raheny) 5		

Grange Rd. 14	54	H16
Grangegorman Lwr. 7	43	J8
Grangegorman Upper 7	35	J7
Grangemore Av. 5	27	S2
Grangemore Ct. 5	27	S2
Rosapenna Dr.		
Grangemore Gro. 5	27	S2
Grangemore Pk. 5	27	S2
Rosapenna Dr.		
Grangemore Ri. 5	27	S2
Rosapenna Dr.		
Granite Pl. 4	51	N11
Granite Ter. 8	41	E9
Inchicore Ter. S.		
Grantham Pl. 8	43	K10
Grantham St. 8	43	K10
Grants Row 2	44	M9
Grattan Ct. E. 2	44	M9
Grattan St.		
Grattan Cres. 8	41	E9
Grattan Par. 9	35	K6
Grattan Pl. 2	44	M9
Grattan St.		
Grattan St. 2	44	M9
Gray Sq. 8	43	J9
Pimlico		
Gray St. 8	43	J9
Great Clarence Pl. 2	44	M9
Great Western Av. 7	35	J7
North Circular Rd.		
Great Western Sq. 7	35	J7
Great Western Vills. 7	35	J7
Greek St. 7	43	J8
Green Pk. 14	55	K14
Green Rd., D.L.	58	Q15
Green St. 7	43	J8
Green St. E. 2	45	N9
Green St. Little 7	43	J8
Greenacre Ct. 14	53	E16
Greencastle Av. 5	26	P2
Greencastle Cres. 5	26	P2
Greencastle Dr. 5	26	P2
Greencastle Par. 5	26	Q2
Greendale Av. 5	28	T3
Greendale Rd. 5	28	T3
Greenfield Cres. 4	51	N13
Greenfield Pk. 4	51	N13
Greenfield Rd., Howth	30	X2
Greenfield Rd., Stillorgan	58	P15
Greenhills Rd., Tallaght	52	C15
Greenlea Av. 6	54	G14
Greenlea Dr. 6	54	G14
Greenlea Gro. 6	54	G14
Greenlea Pk. 6	54	G14
Greenlea Rd. 6	54	G14
Greenmount Av. 12	49	J11
Greenmount Ct. 12	49	J11
Greenmount Av.		
Greenmount La. 12	49	J11
Greenmount Lawns 6	54	H14
Greenmount Rd. 6	49	J13
Greenmount Sq. 12	49	J11
Greenmount La.		
Greenore Ter. 2	44	M9
Greentrees Dr. 12	53	E14
Greentrees Pk. 12	47	E13
Greentrees Rd. 12	53	E14
Greenville Av. 8	43	J10
Greenville Rd., D.L.	59	S16
Greenville Ter. 8	43	J10
Grenville La. 1	35	K7
Grenville St. 1	35	K7
Gresham Ter., D.L.	61	V16
Greygates, D.L.	58	P15
Greyhound Race Track 6	49	J12
Greys La., Howth	31	BB4
Griffith Av. 9	23	K4
Griffith Av. Ext. 11	23	J4
Griffith Ct. 9	36	M5

Griffith Downs 9	24	L4
Griffith Dr. 11	22	H3
Griffith Lawns 9	23	K4
Griffith Par. 11	22	H4
Griffith Sq. 8	49	J11
Wesley Pl.		
Griffith Sq. S. 8	43	J10
South Circular Rd.		
Grosvenor Ct. 3	38	P5
Grosvenor Ct. 12	53	F14
Grosvenor Pk. 6	49	J12
Grosvenor Pl. 6	49	J12
Grosvenor Rd. 6	49	J12
Grosvenor Sq. 6	49	J11
Grosvenor Ter., D.L.	60	U16
Grosvenor Vills. 6	49	J12
Grotto Av., Booterstown	58	P14
Grotto Pl., Booterstown	58	P14
Grove, The 5	27	S4
Grove, The 9	24	M4
Grove Av. 6	49	J11
Grove Rd.		
Grove Av. (Finglas) 11	22	H2
Grove Av., Blackrock	58	Q15
Grove Lawn, Stillorgan	58	Q15
Grove Pk. 6	49	K11
Grove Pk. Av. 11	22	H2
Grove Pk. Cres. 11	23	J2
Grove Pk. Dr. 11	22	H2
Grove Pk. Rd. 11	22	H2
Grove Rd.	49	J11
(Rathmines) 6		
Grove Rd. (Finglas) 11	22	H2
Growewood 11	22	H2
Guild St. 1	44	M8
Guinness Brewery 8	42	H9
Gulistan Cotts. 6	49	K11
Gulistan Pl. 6	49	K12
Gulistan Ter. 6	49	K11
H.S. Reilly Bri. 11	33	F5
Haddington Pl. 4	44	M10
Haddington Rd. 4	44	M10
Haddington Ter., D.L.	61	V16
Haddon Pk. 3	37	O6
Seaview Av. N.		
Haddon Rd. 3	37	O6
Hagans Ct. 2	44	L10
Haigh Ter., D.L.	61	V16
Halliday Rd. 7	42	H8
Halliday Sq. 7	42	H8
Halston St. 7	43	J8
Hamilton St. 8	42	H10
Hammond La. 7	43	J8
Hammond St. 8	43	J10
Hampstead Av. 9	23	K4
Hampstead Ct. 9	23	K3
Hampstead Pk. 9	23	K3
Hampton Convent 9	36	M5
Hampton Cres., D.L.	58	P14
Hampton Est. 3	38	Q5
Hampton Pk., D.L.	58	P15
Hanbury La. 8	43	J9
Hannaville Pk. 6	48	H13
Hanover La. 8	43	J9
Hanover Quay 2	44	M9
Hanover Sq. W. 8	43	J9
Hanover La.		
Hanover St. E. 2	44	L9
Hanover St. W. 8	43	J9
Ash St.		
Harbour Ct. 1	43	K8
Marlborough St.		
Harbour Rd., Howth	31	AA2
Harbour Ter., D.L.	60	U15
Harbour Vw., Howth	31	BB3
St. Lawrence Rd.		
Harcourt La. 2	43	K10
Harcourt Rd.		
Harcourt Rd. 2	43	K10
Harcourt St. 2	43	K10

Harcourt Ter. 2	44	L10
Killarney St.		
Hardbeck Av. 12	46	D12
Hardiman Rd. 9	35	K5
Hardwicke Pl. 1	35	K7
Hardwicke St. 1	35	K7
Harlech Cres. 14	57	N15
Harlech Downs 14	57	N15
Harlech Gro. 14	57	N15
Harlech Vills. 14	57	N15
Harman St. 8	42	H10
Harmonstown Gro. 5	26	Q4
Harmonstown Rd. 5	26	Q4
Harmony Av. 4	50	M12
Harmony Row 2	44	M9
Harold Rd. 7	42	H8
Harolds Cross 6	49	J11
Harolds Cross Rd. 6	48	H13
Haroldville Av. 8	42	H10
Harrington St. 8	43	K10
Harrison Row 6	49	J13
Harry St. 2	43	K9
Harty Av. 12	47	E12
Harty Pl. 8	43	J10
Harvard 14	57	N15
Hastings St. 4	45	N9
Hatch La. 2	44	L10
Hatch St. Lwr. 2	44	L10
Hatch St. Upper 2	43	K10
Havelock Sq. E. 4	45	N10
Havelock Sq. N. 4	45	N10
Havelock Sq. S. 4	45	N10
Havelock Sq. W. 4	45	N10
Havelock Ter. 4	45	N10
Bath Av.		
Haven, The 9	23	K4
Haverty Rd. 3	37	N6
Hawkins St. 2	44	L8
Hawthorn Av. 3	44	M8
Church Rd.		
Hawthorn Manor, D.L.	59	R16
Hawthorn Ter. 3	36	M7
Haymarket 7	43	J8
Hazel Pk. 12	48	G13
Hazel Rd. 9	37	N5
Hazelbrook Dr. 6	48	G13
Hazelbrook Rd. 6	48	G13
Hazelcroft Gdns. 11	22	G4
Hazelcroft Rd.		
Hazelcroft Pk. 11	22	G4
Hazelcroft Rd.		
Hazelcroft Rd. 11	22	G4
Hazeldean 4	51	N12
Hazelwood Ct. 9	25	O2
Hazelwood Dr. 5	25	O3
Hazelwood Gro. 5	25	O3
Hazelwood Pk. 5	25	O3
Headford Gro. 14	55	K16
Healthfield Rd. 6	49	J13
Healy St. 1	36	L7
Rutland Pl. N.		
Heath Cres. 7	33	E5
Heath Gro. 7	33	F5
Heidelberg 14	57	N15
Hendrick La. 7	42	H8
Benburb St.		
Hendrick Pl. 8	42	H8
Hendrick St. 7	43	J8
Henley Pk. 14	56	L15
Henley Vills. 14	56	L15
Henrietta La. 1	43	K8
Henrietta Pl. 1	43	J8
Henrietta St. 1	43	J8
Henry Pl. 1	43	K8
Henry St. 1	43	K8
Herbert Av. 4	63	P13
Herbert Cotts. 4	51	N11
Herbert La. 2	44	M10
Herbert St.		
Herbert Pk. 4	50	M11
Herbert Pl. 2	44	M10
Herbert Rd. 4	45	N10
Herbert St. 2	44	L10
Herberton Dr. 12	42	G10
Herberton Pk. 8	42	G10
Heuston Sta. 8	42	G8

Hewardine Ter. 1	36	L7
Killarney St.		
Heytesbury La. 4	50	M11
Heytesbury Pl. 8	43	J10
Long La.		
Heytesbury St. 8	43	K10
Hibernian Av. 3	36	M7
Hibernian Marino Sch. 3	39	R6
High Pk. 9	24	M4
High Sch. of Domestic Economy, D.L.	58	Q14
High St. 8	43	J9
Highfield Ct. 6	49	J13
Highfield Gro. 6	49	K13
Highfield Pk. 14	56	L15
Highfield Rd. 6	49	J13
Highthorn Pk., D.L.	60	U17
Hill, The, D.L.	60	U16
Hill St. 1	35	K7
Hillcrest Pk. 11	23	J3
Hillsbrook Av. 12	47	E13
Hillsbrook Cres. 12	47	E13
Hillsbrook Dr. 12	47	F13
Hillsbrook Gro. 12	47	E13
Hillside Dr. 14	55	J15
Hillside Vw., Howth	28	U3
Hoeys Ct. 2	43	K9
Castle St.		
Hogan Av. 2	44	M9
Hogan Pl. 2	44	M9
Holles Row 2	44	M9
Holles St. 2	44	L9
Holly Rd. 9	37	N5
Hollybank Av. 6	50	L12
Hollybank Rd. 9	35	K6
Hollybrook Ct. 3	37	O6
Hollybrook Rd.		
Hollybrook Ct. Dr. 3	37	O6
Hollybrook Rd.		
Hollybrook Gro. 3	37	N6
Hollybrook Pk. 3	37	O6
Hollybrook Rd. 3	37	O6
Hollywood Dr. 14	57	N16
Hollywood Pk. 14	57	N16
Holmston Av., D.L.	61	V17
Holy Cross Coll. 3	36	L6
Holycross Av. 3	36	L6
Holylands Dr. 14	55	K16
Holyrood Pk. 4	51	O11
Holywell Cres. 5	27	S2
Holywell Rd. 5	27	S2
Home Fm. Pk. 9	36	L5
Home Fm. Rd. 9	23	K4
Home Vills. 4	50	M11
Homeville 6	49	K12
Hope Av. 3	36	M7
Hope St. 4	44	M9
Horseman's Row 1	43	K8
Parnell St.		
Horton Ct. 6	54	H14
Hospital for Incurables 4	50	L11
Hotel Yd. 1	43	K8
House of Retreat 8	41	E10
Howard St. 4	44	M9
Howth Castle, Howth	31	AA3
Howth Golf Course, Howth	30	Z4
Howth Rd. 3	37	N6
Howth Rd., Howth	30	Z2
Howth Sta., Howth	31	AA2
Howth Vw. Pk. 5	27	S2
Huband Bri. 4	44	M10
Huband Rd. 12	46	D11
Hudson Rd., D.L.	61	W17
Hughes Rd. E. 12	47	E12
Hughes Rd. N. 12	47	E12
Hughes Rd. S. 12	47	E12
Hume St. 2	44	L10
Huttons Pl. 1	36	L7
Huxley Cres. 8	42	H10
Hyacinth St. 3	36	M7
Hyde Pk. 6	54	G15
Hyde Pk. Av., D.L.	58	Q15

71

Hyde Pk. Gdns., Blackrock	58 Q15	Joyce Rd. 9	35 K5
		Jumping Grd. 4	51 N11
Idrone Ter., D.L.	59 R15	Keadeen Av., Tallaght	52 C14
Imaal Rd. 7	34 H6	Kearns Pl. 8	42 G9
Inchicore Rd. 8	41 F9	Keeper Rd. 12	42 G10
Inchicore Sq. 8	41 E9	Kells Rd. 12	48 G12
Inchicore Ter. N. 8	41 E9	Kelly's Av., D.L.	60 U15
Inchicore Ter. S. 8	41 E9	Kelly's Row 1	35 K7
Incorporated Dental Hosp. of Ireland 2	44 L9	Dorset St. Lwr.	
		Kempton Av. 7	33 E5
Incorporated Orthopaedic Hosp. 3	38 P6	Kempton Grn. 7	33 E5
		Kempton Gro. 7	33 E5
Infirmary Rd. 7	42 G8	Kempton Ri. 7	33 E5
Ingram Rd. 3	43 J10	Kempton Way 7	33 E5
Innisfallen Par. 7	35 K6	Kenilworth Pk. 6	48 H12
Innishmaan Rd. 9	24 L4	Kenilworth Rd. 6	49 J12
Inns Quay 8	43 J9	Kenilworth Sq. E. 6	49 J12
Inver Rd. 7	34 G6	Kenilworth Sq. N. 6	49 J12
Invermore Gro. 5	27 S2	Kenilworth Sq. S. 6	49 J12
Carraroe Av.		Kenilworth Sq. W. 6	49 J12
Inverness Rd. 3	36 M6	Kenmare Par. 1	35 K7
Iona Cres. 9	35 K6	Dorset St. Lwr.	
Iona Dr. 9	35 K6	Kennedys Vills. 8	42 G9
Iona Pk. 9	35 K6	Kennington Clo.,	52 D15
Iona Rd. 9	35 J6	Tallaght	
Iona Vills. 9	35 K6	Kennington Cres.,	52 D15
Iris Gro., Stillorgan	57 O15	Tallaght	
Irishtown Rd. 4	45 N9	Kennington Lawn,	53 E15
Irvine Cres. 3	44 M8	Tallaght	
Church Rd.		Kennington Rd.,	52 D15
Irvine Ter. 3	44 M8	Tallaght	
Irwin St. 8	42 G9	Keogh Sq. 8	41 F9
Island St. 8	42 H9	Kerlogue Rd. 4	45 O10
Island Vill. 2	44 M9	Kevin St. Lwr. 8	43 K10
Hogan Av.		Kevin St. Upper 8	43 J10
Islington Av., D.L.	61 V16	Kickam Rd. 8	41 F9
Isolda Rd. 4	45 O9	Kilakea Clo. 12	52 C14
Ivar St. 7	42 H8	Tibradden Dr.	
Iveagh Bldgs. 8	43 J10	Kilakea Dr. 12	52 C14
Iveagh Gdns. 12	47 F11	Tibradden Dr.	
Iveleary Rd. 9	24 L4	Kilbarrack Av. 5	28 U3
Iveragh Rd. 9	24 L3	Kilbarrack Gdns. 5	28 U3
Ivy Ter. 8	42 H10	Kilbarrack Gro. 5	28 T3
		Kilbarrack Rd. 5	27 S2
James Joyce St. 1	28 U3	Kilbarron Av. 5	25 N2
Kilbarrack		Kilbarron Dr. 5	25 N2
James Larkin Rd. 5	39 S5	Kilbarron Pk. 5	25 N2
James McCormack Gdns., Sutton	29 W2	Kilbarron Rd. 5	25 N2
		Kilbride Rd. 5	38 P5
James Pl. E. 2	44 L10	Kildare Pk. 12	47 F11
James St. N. 3	36 M7	Kildare Rd. 12	47 F11
James's Gate 8	42 H9	Kildare St. 2	44 L9
James's St.		Kildonan Av. 11	21 F2
James's St. 8	42 H9	Kildonan Dr. 11	21 F2
James's St. E. 2	44 L10	Kildonan Rd. 11	21 F2
Jamestown Av. 8	40 D10	Kilfenora Dr. 5	27 S2
Jamestown Rd. (Inchicore) 8	40 D10	Kilfenora Rd. 12	48 G12
		Kilkieran Ct. 7	34 G5
Jamestown Rd. (Finglas) 11	22 G2	Kilkieran Rd. 7	34 G5
		Kill Abbey, D.L.	60 S17
Jane Ville 8	43 J10	Killala Rd. 7	34 G5
Jervis La. Lwr. 1	43 K8	Killan Rd. 3	44 M8
Jervis La. Upper 1	43 K8	Killarney Av. 1	36 L7
Jervis St. 1	43 K8	Killarney Par. 7	35 K6
Jervis St. Hosp. 1	43 K8	Killarney St. 1	36 L7
Jetty Rd. 1	62 P8	Killary Gro. 5	27 S2
John Dillon St. 8	43 J9	Ardara Av.	
John F. Kennedy Dr. 12	46 C11	Killeen Rd. 6	49 K12
		Killester Abbey 5	26 P4
John McCormack Av. 12	47 E12	Killester Av. 5	25 O4
		Killester Pk. 5	26 P4
John St. S. 8	43 J9	Killester Sta. 5	38 P5
John St. W. 8	43 J9	Kilmacud Pk., Stillorgan	57 O16
Johns La. W. 8	43 J9		
Johnsons Ct. 2	43 K9	Kilmacud Rd. Lwr. 14	57 N16
Grafton St.		Kilmacud Rd. Upper 14	56 M16
Johnsons Pl. 2	43 K9		
King St. S.		Kilmainham Bri. 8	41 F9
Johnstown Pk. 11	23 J3	Kilmainham La. 8	41 F9
Jones's Rd. 3	36 L7	Kilmashogue Clo. 12	52 D14
Josephine Av. 7	35 K7	Kilmashogue Dr.	
Leo St.		Kilmashogue Dr. 12	52 D14
Joy St. 4	44 M9	Kilmashogue Gro. 12	52 C14
Barrow St.		Kilmore Av. 5	25 O2
Kilmore Clo. 5	25 O2	Langrishe Pl. 1	36 L7
Kilmore Cres. 5	26 P2	Summerhill	
Kilmore Dr. 5	25 O2	Lansdowne Gdns. 4	45 N10
Kilmore Rd. 5	25 O3	Shelbourne Rd.	
Kilmorony Clo. 5	27 S2	Lansdowne Hall 4	45 N10
Kilmanagh Rd. 12	46 D12	Tritonville Rd.	
Kilohan Gro. 12	52 D14	Lansdowne La. 4	45 N10
Kilshane Rd. 11	21 E3	Lansdowne Pk. 4	44 M10
Kilvere 14	54 G15	Lansdowne Rd. 4	44 M10
Kilworth Rd. 12	47 E11	Lansdowne Rd. Sta. 4	45 N10
Kimmage Ct. 6	48 G13		
Kimmage Cross Rds. 6	48 G13	Lansdowne Ter. 4	51 N11
		Serpentine Av.	
Kimmage Gro. 6	48 H13	Lansdowne Valley Rd. 12	46 D11
Kimmage Rd. Lwr. 6	48 G13		
Kimmage Rd. W. 12	47 F13	Lansdowne Village 4	45 N10
Kinahan St. 7	42 G8	Laracor Gdns. 5	27 S2
Kincora Av. 3	37 O6	Laragh Clo. 5	27 S2
Kincora Ct. 3	38 Q7	Laragh Gro. 5	27 S2
Kincora Dr. 3	38 P6	Laragh Clo.	
Kincora Gro. 3	38 P6	Larch Gro. 6	50 L12
Kincora Pk. 3	38 P6	Larchfield 14	56 L15
Kincora Rd. 3	38 P6	Larchfield Pk. 14	56 M15
King St. N. 7	43 J8	Larchfield Rd. 14	56 M15
King St. S. 2	43 K9	Larkfield Av. 6	48 H12
Kingram La. 2	44 L10	Larkfield Gdns. 6	48 H12
Kings Av. 1	36 M7	Larkfield Gro. 6	48 H12
Kings Hosp. Sch. 8	42 H8	Larkfield Pk. 6	48 H12
Kings Inns St. 1	43 K8	Larkhill Rd. 9	24 L3
Kingsbridge 8	42 H8	Lauders La.,	29 X2
Kingsland Par. 8	49 K11	Baldoyle	
Kingsland Pk. Av. 8	43 K10	Laundry La. 6	49 J12
Kinvara Av. 7	33 F5	Laurel Av. 14	56 L16
Kinvara Dr. 7	33 E5	Laurel Dr. 14	56 L16
Kinvara Gro. 7	33 E5	Laurel La. 14	56 L16
Kinvara Pk. 7	33 E5	Laurels, The 6	48 H13
Kinvara Rd. 7	33 E5	Laurels, The 14	56 L16
Kippure Av. 12	52 C14	Laurelton 6	55 J14
Kippure Pk. 11	21 F4	Lavarna Gro. 6	54 G14
Kirkwood 4	51 O11	Lavarna Rd. 6	48 G13
Kirwan St. 7	42 H8	Lavista Av. (Killester) 5	38 P5
Kirwan St. Cotts. 7	42 H8		
Kirwan St.		Lawn, The 11	22 G3
Kitestown Rd., Howth	31 BB4	Lawrence Gro. 3	37 O6
		Le Bas Ter. 6	49 J12
Knapton Rd., D.L.	60 U16	Leinster Rd. W.	
Knights Bri. 3	38 P6	Le Vere Ter. 6	49 J11
Knockcullen Dr. 14	53 F16	Lea Cres. 4	51 O11
Knockcullen Lawn 14	53 F16	Lea Rd. 4	51 O11
Knockcullen Dr.		Leahys Ter. 4	45 O10
Knockcullen Pk. 14	53 F16	Lee Rd. 11	34 H5
Knocklyon Av. 14	53 E16	Leeson Clo. 2	44 L10
Knocklyon Dr. 14	53 F16	Leeson La. 2	44 L10
Knocklyon Pk. 14	53 E16	Leeson Pk. 6	50 L11
Knocknarea Av. 12	47 F11	Leeson Pk. Av. 6	50 L11
Knocknarea Rd. 12	47 E11	Leeson St. Lwr. 2	44 L10
Knocknashee 14	57 N16	Leeson St. Upper 4	50 L11
Kyber Rd. 8	33 E7	Leeson Village 6	50 L11
Kyle-Clare Rd. 4	45 O9	Leicester Av. 6	49 J12
Kylemore Av. 10	40 C10	Leighlin Rd. 12	48 G12
Kylemore Dr. 10	40 C10	Lein Gdns.	26 Q4
Kylemore Pk. N. 10	40 C10	(Gardini Lein) 5	
Kylemore Pk. S. 10	40 C10	Lein Pk. 5	26 Q3
Kylemore Pk. W. 10	40 C10	Lein Rd. 5	26 Q3
Kylemore Rd. 10	40 C9	Leinster Av. 3	36 M7
		Leinster La. 2	44 L9
La Touche Dr. 12	40 D10	Leinster St. S.	
La Touche Rd. 12	46 D11	Leinster Mkt. 2	43 K8
La Vista Av., Howth	30 Y4	D'Olier St.	
Laburnam Rd. 14	50 M13	Leinster Pl. 6	49 J12
Lad La. 2	44 L10	Leinster Rd. 6	49 J12
Lagan Rd. 11	22 G4	Leinster Rd. W. 6	49 J12
Lakelands Pk. 6	54 H14	Leinster Sq. 6	49 K12
Lally Rd. 10	40 D9	Leinster St. 2	44 L9
Lambay Rd. 9	23 K4	Leinster St. E. 3	36 M7
Lambourne Village 3	38 P6	Leinster St. N. 7	35 J6
Lambs Ct. 8	42 H9	Leinster St. S. 2	44 L9
James's St.		Leitrim Pl. 2	44 M10
Landen Rd. 10	40 C10	Grand Canal St. Upper	
Landscape Av. 14	55 K15	Leix Rd. 7	34 H6
Landscape Cres. 14	55 K15	Leland Pl. 1	44 M8
Landscape Gdns. 14	55 K15	Lemon St. 2	43 K9
Landscape Pk. 14	55 K15	Lennox Pl. 8	49 K11
Landscape Rd. 14	55 K14	Lennox St. 8	49 K11
Lanesville, D.L.	60 T17	Lentisk Lawn 5	27 S2

Oakwood Pk. 11 22 H2
O'Brien Rd. 12 47 E12
O'Brien's Institute 3 37 N5
O'Brien's Pl. N. 9 35 K5
O'Brien's Ter. 9 35 J6
Prospect Rd.
Observatory La. 6 49 K11
Rathmines Rd. Lwr.
O'Carolan Rd. 8 43 J10
Ocean Pier 1 45 O8
O'Connell Av. 7 35 J7
O'Connell Gdns. 4 45 N10
O'Connell St. Lwr. 1 43 K8
O'Connell St. 43 K8
Upper 1
O'Curry Av. 8 43 J10
O'Curry Rd. 8 43 J10
O'Daly Rd. 9 35 K5
Odd Lamp Rd. 8 33 E6
O'Devaney Gdns. 7 42 G8
O'Donnell Gdns., D.L. 61 V17
O'Donoghue St. 8 41 E10
O'Donovan Rd. 8 43 J10
O'Donovan Rossa 43 J9
Bri. 8
O'Dwyer Rd. 12 47 E12
Offaly Rd. 7 34 H6
Offington Av., Howth 30 Y3
Offington Ct., Howth 30 Y3
Offington Dr., Howth 30 Y3
Offington Lawn, 30 Y3
Howth
Offington Pk., Howth 30 Y2
O'Hogan Rd. 10 40 D9
Olaf Rd. 7 42 H8
Old Bri. Rd. 14 53 F15
Old Cabra Rd. 7 34 G6
Old Camden St. 2 43 K10
Harcourt Rd.
Old County Rd. 12 47 F11
Old Dunleary, D.L. 60 U16
Old Kilmainham 8 42 G9
Old Mill Ct. 8 43 J10
Old Mountpleasant 6 49 K11
Mountpleasant Pl.
Old Naas Rd. 12 46 C11
Old Rectory Pk. 14 56 M16
Oldtown Av. 9 23 K2
Oldtown Pk. 9 23 K2
Oldtown Rd. 9 24 L2
O'Leary Rd. 8 47 F10
Olivemount Gro. 14 56 M14
Olivemount Rd. 14 56 M14
Oliver Bond St. 8 43 J9
Oliver Plunkett Av. 45 N9
(Irishtown) 4
Oliver Plunkett Av., 60 T17
D.L.
Oliver Plunkett Cres., 60 T17
D.L.
Oliver Plunkett Av.
Oliver Plunkett Rd., 60 T17
D.L.
Oliver Plunkett Ter., 60 T17
D.L.
Oliver Plunkett Av.
Oliver Plunkett Vills., 60 T17
D.L.
Olney Cres. 6 54 H14
Omni Pk. 9 24 L2
O'Moore Rd. 10 40 D9
O'Neachtain Rd. 9 35 K5
O'Neill's Bldgs. 8 43 K10
Ontario Ter. 6 49 K11
Ophaly Ct. 14 56 M15
O'Quinn Av. 8 42 G9
O'Rahilly Par. 1 43 K8
Moore St.
Orchard, The 5 38 P5
Orchard La., D.L. 59 R16
Orchard Rd. 5 28 T4
Orchard Rd. S. 6 49 K13
Orchardston 14 54 H15
Orchardstown Av. 14 54 G16
Orchardstown Dr. 14 53 F16
Orchardstown Pk. 14 54 G16

Orchardstown Vills. 54 G16
14
Ordnance Survey 32 C6
Office, Castleknock
Ordnance Survey Rd., 32 C6
Castleknock
O'Reilly's Av. 8 42 G9
Oriel Pl. 1 36 M7
Oriel St. Lwr. 1 44 M8
Oriel St. Upper 1 44 M8
Ormeau St. 4 45 N9
Ormond Mkt. Sq. 7 43 J9
Ormond Quay Upper
Ormond Quay Lwr. 1 43 K8
Ormond Quay 43 J9
Upper 7
Ormond Rd. 9 36 L5
Ormond Rd. N. 9 36 L5
Ormond Rd. S. 49 K12
(Rathmines) 6
Ormond Sq. 7 43 J8
Ormond St. 8 43 J10
Orwell Gdns. 14 55 K14
Orwell Pk. 6 55 K14
Orwell Pk. Av. 12 53 E15
Orwell Pk. Clo. 12 53 E15
Orwell Pk. Cres. 12 53 F15
Orwell Pk. Dr. 12 53 F15
Orwell Pk. Glade 2 53 E15
Orwell Pk. Glen 12 53 E15
Orwell Pk. Grn. 12 53 E15
Orwell Pk. Gro. 12 53 E15
Orwell Pk. Lawns 12 53 E15
Orwell Pk. Way 12 53 E15
Orwell Rd. 6 49 J13
Orwell Wds. 6 55 K14
Oscar Sq. 8 43 J10
Osprey Av., Tallaght 53 E14
Osprey Lawn, 53 E14
Tallaght
Osprey Pk., Tallaght 52 D14
Osprey Rd., Tallaght 53 E14
Ossory Rd. 3 36 M7
Ossory Sq. 8 43 J10
Ostman Pl. 7 42 H8
O'Sullivan Av. 3 36 M7
Oswald Rd. 4 45 O10
Otranto Pl., D.L. 61 W17
Oulton Rd. 3 38 P6
Our Lady's Hospice 6 49 J11
Our Lady's Hosp. 12 47 E11
Our Lady's Rd. 8 42 H10
Ovoca Rd. 8 43 J10
Owendoher Av. 14 54 H15
Owendoher Cres. 14 54 H15
Owendore Av. 14 54 H15
Owendore Cres. 14 54 H15
Owens Av. 8 42 G9
Owenstown Pk., 57 O15
Stillorgan
Oxford Rd. 6 49 K11
Oxford Ter. 3 44 M8
Church Rd.
Oxford Ter. 6 49 K11
Oxford Rd.
Oxmantown La. 7 42 H8
Blackhall Pl.
Oxmantown Rd. 7 34 H7
Oxmantown Rd. Lwr. 7 42 H8
Arbour Hill

Pacelli Av., Baldoyle 28 U3
Paddock, The 7 32 D5
Pairc Baile Munna 11 23 J3
Pakenham Rd., D.L. 60 T16
Pakerton, D.L. 60 U16
Sloperton
Palace St. 2 43 K9
Dame St.
Palmerston Gdns. 6 49 K13
Palmerston Gro. 6 50 M13
Palmerston La. 6 50 L13
Palmerston Pk. 6 49 K13
Palmerston Pl. 7 35 J7
Palmerston Rd. 6 49 K12

Palmerston Vills. 6 49 K13
Palms, The 14 57 N15
Paradise Pl. 7 35 K7
Park Av. 4 51 O11
Park Cres. 8 33 F6
Park Cres. 12 53 F13
Park Dr. 6 50 L12
Park La. 4 51 O11
Park La., Chapelizod 40 C8
Park La. E. 2 44 L9
Lincoln Pl.
Park Lawn 3 39 R5
Park Pl. 8 41 F9
South Circular Rd.
Park Rd. 7 33 E5
Park Rd., D.L. 61 V16
Park St. 10 41 E9
Park Ter. 8 43 J9
Park Vw., 32 C5
Castleknock
Park Vw. Av. 6 49 K12
Parkgate St. 8 42 H8
Parkmore Dr. 6 54 G14
Parkvale, Howth 29 V2
Parkview 7 34 G7
Parkview Av. 6 49 J12
Parliament Row 2 43 K9
Fleet St.
Parliament St. 2 43 K9
Parnell Av. 12 49 J11
Parnell Ct. 12 49 J11
Parnell Pl. 1 35 K7
Parnell Rd. 12 42 H10
Parnell Sq. E. 1 35 K7
Parnell Sq. N. 1 35 K7
Parnell Sq. W. 1 43 K8
Parnell St. 1 43 K8
Partridge Ter. 8 40 D10
Patrician Pk., D.L. 60 T17
Patrician Vills., 58 Q16
Stillorgan
Patrick Doyle Rd. 14 56 L14
Patrick St. 8 43 J9
Patrick St., D.L. 60 T16
Patricks Clo. S. 8 43 J9
Patricks Row, D.L. 59 R15
Carysfort Av.
Patrickswell Pl. 1 22 G3
Patriotic Ter. 8 42 G9
Brookfield Rd.
Pea Fld., D.L. 58 Q15
Pearse Gro. 2 44 M9
Great Clarence Pl.
Pearse Ho. 2 44 L9
Pearse Sq. E. 2 44 M9
Pearse Sq. N. 2 44 M9
Pearse Sq. W. 2 44 M9
Pearse Sta. 2 44 L9
Pearse St. 2 44 L9
Pembroke Cotts. 45 N9
(Ringsend)
Pembroke Cotts. 50 M12
(Donnybrook) 14
Pembroke Cotts. 56 M16
(Dundrum) 14
Pembroke Cotts., D.L. 58 P14
Pembroke Gdns. 4 44 M10
Pembroke La. 2 44 L10
Pembroke La. 4 44 M10
Pembroke Pk. 4 50 M11
Pembroke Pl. 2 44 L10
Pembroke St. Upper
Pembroke Pl. 4 51 N11
Herbert Pk.
Pembroke Rd. 4 44 M10
Pembroke Row 2 44 L10
Pembroke St. 4 45 N9
Pembroke St. Lwr. 2 44 L10
Pembroke St. Upper 2 44 L10
Penrose St. 4 45 N9
Percy French Rd. 12 47 E12
Percy La. 4 44 M10
Percy Pl. 4 44 M10
Peter Row 8 43 K9
Peter St. 8 43 K9

Peters Pl. 2 43 K10
Petersons Ct. 2 44 L8
Petrie Rd. 8 43 J10
Phibsborough 7 35 J7
Phibsborough Av. 7 35 J7
Phibsborough Pl. 7 35 J7
Phibsborough Rd. 7 35 J7
Philipsburgh Av. 3 36 M6
Philipsburgh Ter. 3 36 M6
Philomena Ter. 4 45 N9
Phoenix Manor 7 34 G7
Phoenix St. 7 43 J8
Phoenix St. 10 41 E9
Phoenix Ter., D.L. 58 Q14
Pig La. 1 36 L7
Pigeon Ho. Rd. 4 45 O10
Piles Bldgs. 8 43 K9
Golden La.
Piles Ter. 2 44 L9
Pim St. 8 42 H9
Pimlico 8 43 J9
Pimlico Sq. 8 43 J9
The Coombe
Pine Haven, D.L. 58 Q14
Pine Hurst 7 34 G6
Pine Rd. 4 45 O9
Pinebrook Av. 5 25 O4
Pinebrook Cres. 5 25 O4
Pinebrook Av.
Pinebrook Gro. 5 25 O4
Pinebrook Rd.
Pinebrook Ri. 5 25 O4
Pinebrook Rd. 5 25 O4
Pines, The 5 26 P4
Pinewood Av. 11 23 J2
Pinewood Cres. 11 23 J2
Pinewood Dr. 11 23 J2
Pinewood Grn. 11 23 J2
Pinewood Gro. 11 23 J2
Pinewood Pk. 14 54 G16
Pinewood Vills. 11 23 J2
Pleasants La. 8 43 K10
Pleasants Pl. 8 43 K10
Pleasants St. 8 43 K10
Plunkett Grn. 11 21 F2
Plunkett Rd. 11 21 F2
Poddle Pk. 12 48 G13
Polo Rd. 8 33 F7
Poolbeg St. 2 44 L8
Poole St. 8 43 J9
Poplar Row 3 36 M6
Poplars, The, D.L. 60 T16
Portland Clo. 1 36 L7
Portland Pl. 1 35 K6
Portland Row 1 36 L7
Portland Row N. 1 36 L7
Portland St. 8 42 H9
Portland St. N. 1 36 L7
Portmahon Dr. 8 42 G10
Portobello Barracks 6 49 J11
Portobello Bri. 6 49 K11
Portobello Harbour 8 49 K11
Portobello Pl. 8 49 K11
Portobello Rd. 8 49 J11
Portobello Sq. 8 49 J11
Clanbrassil St. Upper
Potato Mkt. 7 43 J8
Green St. Little
Potters All. 1 44 L8
Powers Ct. 2 44 M10
Powers Sq. 8 43 J9
John Dillon St.
Prebend St. 7 43 J8
Preston St. 1 43 J8
Prices La. 2 43 K8
Prices La. 6 49 K11
Priestfield Cotts. 8 42 H10
Priestfield Dr. 8 42 H10
South Circular Rd.
Priestfield Ter. 8 42 H10
South Circular Rd.
Primrose Av. 7 35 J7
Primrose St. 7 35 J7
Prince Arthur Ter. 6 49 K12
Prince of Wales Ter. 4 51 N11

75

Sarto Pk., Kilbarrack 28 U2
Sarto Rd., Kilbarrack 28 U3
Saul Rd. 12 48 G11
School Av. 5 26 P4
School Ho. La. W. 8 43 J9
School St. 8 42 H9
Schoolhouse La. 2 44 L9
Sea Vw. Ter. 4 51 N12
Seabank Ct., D.L. 61 W17
Seabury 4 63 P12
Seacliff Av., Baldoyle 29 V2
Seacliff Dr., Baldoyle 28 U2
Seacourt 3 39 R6
Seafield Av. 3 38 Q6
Seafield Av., D.L. 60 T16
Seafield Clo., Stillorgan 57 O14
Seafield Ct., Howth 29 W2
Seafield Cres., Stillorgan 58 P14
Seafield Down 3 39 R6
Seafield Dr., Booterstown 58 P14
Seafield Gro. 3 39 R6
Seafield Pk., Booterstown 58 P14
Seafield Rd. 4 57 O14
Seafield Rd. E. 3 38 Q6
Seafield Rd. W. 3 38 P6
Seafort Av. 4 45 O10
Seafort Cotts. 4 45 O10
Seafort Av.
Seafort Gdns. 4 45 O10
Seafort Vills. 4 45 O10
Seafort Av.
Seagrange Av., Baldoyle 28 U2
Seagrange Dr., Baldoyle 29 V2
Seagrange Rd., Baldoyle 28 U2
Sean Heuston Bri. 8 42 H8
Sean McDermott St. Lwr. 1 36 L7
Sean McDermott St. Upper 1 43 K8
Sean More Rd. 4 45 O10
Sean O'Casey La. 1 36 L7
Seapark Dr. 3 38 Q6
Seapark Rd. 3 38 Q6
Seapoint Av., D.L. 59 S15
Seaview Av. E. 3 36 M7
Seaview Av. N. 3 37 O6
Seaview Ter., Howth 31 BB3
Second Av. 1 44 M8
Second Av. (Rialto) 8 42 G10
Selskar Ter. 6 49 K11
Serpentine Av. 4 51 N11
Serpentine Pk. 4 45 N10
Serpentine Rd. 4 45 N10
Serpentine Ter. 4 51 N11
Seven Oaks 9 24 L4
Seventh Av. 8 42 G10
Seville Pl. 1 44 M8
Seville Ter. 1 36 M7
Shamrock Cotts. 1 36 M7
Shamrock Pl.
Shamrock Pl. 1 36 M7
Shamrock St. 7 35 J7
Primrose St.
Shamrock Ter. 1 36 M7
Shamrock Vills. 6 49 J12
Shanard Av. 9 23 K3
Shanard Rd. 9 24 L2
Shanboley Rd. 9 24 M2
Shandon Cres. 7 35 J6
Shandon Dr. 7 35 J6
Shandon Gdns. 7 34 H6
Shandon Pk. 7 35 J6
Shandon Pk., D.L. 59 S15
Shandon Rd. 7 35 J6
Shangan Av. 9 24 L2
Shangan Gdns. 9 24 L2
Shangan Grn. 9 24 L2

Shangan Pk. 9 24 L2
Shangan Rd. 9 23 K2
Shangangh Rd. 9 35 K6
Shanglas Rd. 9 24 M3
Shanid Rd. 6 48 H13
Shanliss Av. 9 24 L2
Shanliss Dr. 9 24 L2
Shanliss Gro. 9 24 L2
Shanliss Pk. 9 24 L2
Shanliss Rd. 9 24 L2
Shanliss Wk. 9 24 L2
Shanliss Way 9 24 L2
Shannon Ter. 8 42 G9
Shanowen Av. 9 24 L3
Shanowen Cres. 9 24 L2
Shanowen Dr. 9 24 L3
Shanowen Gro. 9 23 K2
Shanowen Pk. 9 23 K3
Shanowen Rd. 9 24 L3
Shanrath Rd. 9 24 M3
Shantalla Av. 9 24 M3
Shantalla Dr. 9 24 M3
Shantalla Pk. 9 24 M3
Shantalla Rd. 9 24 M3
Shanvarna Rd. 9 24 M3
Shaw St. 2 44 L9
Shaws La. 4 45 N10
Shelbourne Av. 4 51 N11
Shelbourne Rd.
Shelbourne La. 4 51 N11
Shelbourne Pk. 45 N9
Greyhound Race Course 4
Shelbourne Rd. 4 45 N10
Shelmalier Rd. 3 36 M7
Shelmartin Av. 3 36 M6
Shelmartin Ter. 3 36 M6
Shelton Dr. 12 47 F13
Shelton Gdns. 2 47 F13
Shelton Gro. 12 47 F13
Shelton Pk. 12 47 F13
Sheriff St. Lwr. 1 44 L8
Sheriff St. Upper 1 44 M8
Sherkin Gdns. 9 24 L4
Sherrard Av. 1 35 K7
Sherrard St. Lwr. 1 35 K7
Sherrard St. Upper 1 35 K7
Shielmartin Dr., Howth 30 Y4
Shielmartin Pk., Howth 30 Y4
Shielmartin Rd., Howth 30 Y4
Ship St. Great 8 43 K9
Ship St. Little 8 43 K9
Shrewsbury 4 51 O11
Shrewsbury Pk. 4 51 O11
Shrewsbury Rd. 4 51 N12
Sigurd Rd. 7 42 H8
Silchester Ct., D.L. 61 V17
Silchester Cres., D.L. 61 V17
Silchester Pk., D.L. 61 V17
Silchester Rd., D.L. 61 V17
Silloge Av. 11 23 J2
Silloge Gdns. 11 23 K2
Silloge Rd. 11 23 J2
Silver Birches 14 56 M16
Silverwood Dr. 6 53 F15
Templeville Dr.
Silverwood Dr. 14 54 G16
Silverwood Rd. 14 54 G16
Simmonscourt 50 M12
(Donnybrook) 4
Simmonscourt Av. 4 51 N12
Simmonscourt Castle 4 51 N12
Simmonscourt Rd. 4 51 N11
Sion Hill Av. 6 48 H12
Sion Hill Rd. 9 24 M4
Sir John Rogersons Quay 2 44 M8
Sir Patrick Duns Hosp. 2 44 M9
Sitric Rd. 7 42 H8
Sixth Av. 8 42 G10

Skellys La. 5 25 N3
Skippers All. 8 43 J9
Skreen Rd. 7 33 F6
Slademore Av. 5 26 Q2
Slademore Clo. 5 27 R2
Slademore Ct. 5 26 Q2
Slademore Dr. 5 27 R2
Slane Rd. 12 48 G11
Slaney Rd. 11 34 H5
Slemish Rd. 7 33 F6
Slieve Rua Dr., Stillorgan 57 O16
Slievebloom Pk. 12 47 E11
Slievebloom Rd. 12 47 E11
Slievemore Rd. 12 47 F11
Slievenamon Rd. 12 42 G10
Sloperton, D.L. 60 U16
Smithfield 7 43 J8
Smiths Vills., D.L. 60 U16
Somerset St. 4 45 N9
Somerville Av. 2 47 E12
Somerville Pk. 12 47 E12
Sommerville 14 56 M15
Sorbonne 14 57 N15
South Av., Stillorgan 58 P16
South Circular Rd. 8 41 E8
South Docks Rd. 4 45 N9
South Great Georges St. 2 43 K9
South Hill 6 50 L13
South Hill, Howth 30 Y4
South Hill Av., D.L. 58 P15
South Hill Pk., D.L. 58 P15
South Lotts Rd. 4 45 N10
South Rd. No. 4 1 62 P8
Southern Cross Av. 8 41 F9
Southwood Pk., D.L. 58 Q15
Spa Rd. (Kilmainham) 8 41 E9
Spa Rd. (Phoenix Pk.) 8 33 F7
Spafield Ter. 4 51 N11
Spencer Av. 1 44 M8
Spencer Dock 1 44 M8
Guild St.
Spencer St. 8 43 J10
South Circular Rd.
Spencer St. N. 3 36 M7
Spencer Vills., D.L. 61 W17
Sperrin Rd. 12 47 E11
Spire Vw. La. 6 49 J12
Spitalfields 8 43 J9
Spring Gdn. St. 3 36 M7
Springdale Rd. 5 26 Q3
Springfield 7 33 F6
Springfield Av. 6 54 G15
Springfield Cres. 6 54 G15
Springfield Dr. 6 54 G15
Springfield Pk. 6 54 G15
Springfield Rd. 6 54 G15
Springhill Pk., Stillorgan 60 S17
Square, The 4 45 N9
Square, The 6 48 H12
Stable La. 2 43 K10
Harcourt St.
Stable La. 4 45 N10
Stables, The, D.L. 58 P14
Stamer St. 8 43 K10
Stanaway Dr. 12 48 G12
Stanford Grn. 12 47 E12
Stannaway Av. 12 47 F12
Stannaway Rd. 12 48 G12
Station Rd. 5 27 R4
Station Rd., Sutton 29 W2
Steevens Hosp. 8 42 H9
Steevens La. 8 42 H9
Stella Av. 9 23 K4
Stephen St. 2 43 K9
Stephen St. Upper 8 43 K9
Stephens La. 2 44 M10
Stephens Pl. 2 44 L10
Stephens Rd. 8 41 F10
Stiles Rd., The 3 37 O6

Stillorgan Pk., Stillorgan 58 Q16
Stillorgan Pk. Av., Stillorgan 58 Q16
Stillorgan Rd. (Stillorgan) 4 51 N12
Stirling Pk. 14 55 K14
Stirrup La. 7 43 J8
Beresford St.
Stonepark Abbey 14 55 J16
Stoneview Pl., D.L. 61 V16
Stoney Rd. 3 36 M7
East Wall Rd.
Stoney Rd. (Dundrum) 14 56 M16
Stoneybatter 7 42 H8
Store St. 1 44 L8
Stormanstown Rd. 11 23 J3
Stradbrook, D.L. 59 S16
Stradbrook Clo., Stillorgan 60 S17
Stradbrook Gdns., D.L. 59 S16
Stradbrook Rd.
Stradbrook Hill, Stillorgan 60 S17
Stradbrook Lawn, D.L. 59 S16
Stradbrook Pk., D.L. 59 S16
Stradbrook Rd., D.L. 59 S16
Strand Rd. (Sandymount) 4 51 O11
Strand Rd., Howth 30 Y4
Strand St. 4 45 N9
Strand St. Great 1 43 K8
Strand St. Little 7 43 K8
Strandville Av. E. 3 37 O6
Strandville Av. N. 3 36 M7
Strandville Ho. 3 37 O6
Strangford Gdns. 3 36 M7
Strangford Rd. 3 36 M7
Stratford Row 1 36 L7
Streamville Rd. 5 27 S2
Suffolk St. 2 43 K9
Suir Rd. 8 41 F10
Sullivan St. 7 42 G8
Summer Pl. 1 36 L7
Summer St. N. 1 36 L7
Summer St. S. 8 42 H9
Summerhill 1 36 L7
Summerhill Par. 1 36 L7
Summerhill Pl. 1 36 L7
Summerhill Rd., D.L. 61 V16
Summerville Pk. 6 49 K12
Sunbury Gdns. 6 49 K13
Sundrive Pk. 12 48 H12
Sundrive Rd. 12 48 G11
Sunnyside Ms. 3 38 Q6
Susan Ter. 8 43 J10
Susanville Rd. 3 36 L6
Sussex Rd. 4 50 L11
Sussex St., D.L. 61 V16
Sussex Ter. Lwr. 4 44 L10
Mespil Rd.
Sussex Ter. Upper 4 50 L11
Leeson St. Upper
Sutton Boul. S., Kilbarrack 28 U3
Sutton Ct., Kilbarrack 29 V3
Sutton Downs, Kilbarrack 29 V3
Sutton Gro., Kilbarrack 29 V2
Swan Pl. 4 50 M11
Morehampton Rd.
Swan Yd. 2 43 K9
Harry St.
Swans Nest Av. 5 28 T3
Swans Nest Ct. 5 28 T3
Swans Nest Rd. 5 27 S2
Sweeneys Ter. 8 43 J10
Mill St.
Sweetmans Av., D.L. 59 R15

78

Name	Page	Grid
Sweetmount Av. 14	56	L16
Sweetmount Dr. 14	56	L16
Sweetmount Pk. 14	56	L16
Swifts All. 8	43	J9
Swifts Row 1	43	J9
Ormond Quay Upper		
Swilly Rd. 7	34	G6
Swords Rd. 8	24	L2
Swords Rd. N. 9	24	L4
Swords St. 7	42	H8
Sybil Hill Av. 5	26	Q4
Sybil Hill Rd. 5	26	Q4
Sycamore Cres., Stillorgan	58	P15
Sycamore Pk. 11	22	H2
Sycamore Rd. (Finglas) 11	22	H2
Sycamore Rd., Mount Merrion	58	P15
Sycamore St. 2	43	K9
Sydenham Rd. (Sandymount) 4	51	N11
Sydenham Rd. (Dundrum) 14	56	M16
Sydenham Vills. 14	56	M16
Sydney Av., D.L.	59	R15
Sydney Par. Av. 4	51	O12
Sydney Ter., D.L.	59	R15
Sykes La. 6	49	J13
Synge La. 8	43	K10
Synge Pl. 8	43	K10
Synge St. 8	43	K10
Synnott Pl. 7	35	K7
Synnott Row 7	35	K7
Talbot La. 3	44	L8
Talbot St.		
Talbot Pl. 1	44	L8
Talbot St. 1	44	L8
Tallaght Rd., Tallaght	52	C16
Taney Av. 14	56	M16
Taney Ct. 14	56	M16
Taney Cres. 14	56	M16
Taney Dr. 14	56	M16
Taney Gro. 14	57	N16
Taney Lawn 14	56	M16
Taney Manor 14	56	M16
Taney Pk. 14	56	M16
Taney Ri. 14	56	M16
Taney Rd. 14	56	M16
Tara Hill Cres. 14	54	H16
Tara Hill Gro. 14	54	H16
Tara Hill Rd. 14	54	H16
Tara Lawn 5	27	S2
Tara St. 2	44	L8
Tara St. Sta. 2	44	L8
Taylors La. 8	42	H9
Teach Ultain 2	49	K11
Temple Bar 2	43	K9
Temple Cotts. 7	35	J7
Temple Cres., D.L.	59	S15
Temple Gdns. 6	49	K13
Temple Hill, D.L.	59	S15
Temple La. N. 1	35	K7
Temple La. S. 2	43	K9
Temple Manor Av., Tallaght	52	D14
Temple Manor Clo., Tallaght	52	D14
Temple Manor Ct., Tallaght	52	D14
Temple Manor Dr., Tallaght	52	D14
Temple Manor Gro., Tallaght	52	D14
Temple Manor Way, Tallaght	52	D14
Temple Pk. 6	50	L13
Temple Pk. Av., D.L.	59	S15
Temple Pl. 6	50	L11
Temple Rd. 6	49	K13
Temple Rd., D.L.	59	R15
Temple Sq. 6	49	K13
Temple St. N. 1	35	K7
Temple St. W. 7	42	H8
Temple Vills. 6	49	K12
Palmerston Rd.		
Templemore Av. 6	49	K13
Templeogue Rd. 6	54	G15
Templeogue Wd. 12	53	F15
Templeogue Wd. Heights 12	53	F15
Templeville Av. 6	53	F15
Templeville Dr. 6	53	F15
Templeville Pk. 6	54	G15
Templeville Rd. 6	53	F14
Terenure Coll. 6	54	G14
Terenure Pk. 6	48	H13
Terenure Pl. 6	48	H13
Terenure Rd. E. 6	48	H13
Terenure Rd. N. 6	48	H13
Terenure Rd. W. 6	48	G13
Terminal Rd. N. 1	62	P8
Terminal Rd. S. 1	62	P8
Thatch Rd., The 9	24	M4
Third Av. 1	44	M8
Third Av. 8	42	H10
Dolphin's Barn		
Third Av. (Rialto) 8	42	G10
Thomas St. 8	43	J9
Thomas Davis St. S. 8	43	J9
Thomas Davis St. W. 8	41	E10
Thomas La. 1	43	K8
Thomas Moore Rd. 12	46	D12
Thomas St. E. 4	45	N9
Thomas St. W. 8	42	H9
Thomond Rd. 10	40	C9
Thor Pl. 7	42	H8
Thornanby Lawns, Howth	31	BB3
Thornanby Rd., Howth	31	BB3
Thornanby Wds., Howth	31	BB4
Thorncastle St. 4	45	N9
Thorncliffe Pk. 14	55	K14
Thorndale Av. 5	25	O4
Elm Mt. Rd.		
Thorndale Ct. 9	24	M4
Thorndale Cres. 5	25	O4
Elm Mt. Rd.		
Thorndale Dr. 5	25	O4
Thorndale Gro. 5	25	O4
Thorndale Lawn 5	25	O4
Elm Mt. Rd.		
Thorndale Pk. 5	25	O4
Elm Mt. Rd.		
Thornhill Rd., Stillorgan	57	O16
Thornville Av. 5	28	T3
Thornville Dr. 5	28	T3
Thornville Pk., Kilbarrack	28	T3
Thornville Rd. 5	28	T3
Three Rock Clo. 12	52	C14
Kilmashogue Gro.		
Thundercat All. 7	43	J8
Smithfield		
Tibradden Clo. 12	52	C14
Tibradden Dr.		
Tibradden Dr. 12	52	C14
Tibradden Gro. 12	52	C14
Tibradden Dr.		
Timber Quay 1	45	O8
Tivoli Clo., D.L.	60	U17
Tivoli Rd., D.L.	60	U16
Tivoli Ter. E., D.L.	60	U16
Tivoli Ter. N., D.L.	60	U16
Tivoli Ter. S., D.L.	60	U16
Tolka Cotts. 11	22	H4
Tolka Est. Rd. 11	23	J4
Tolka Quay 1	45	O8
Tolka Quay Rd. 1	62	P8
Tolka Rd. 3	36	L6
Tolka Vw. Ter. 11	22	H4
Tom Clarke Ho. 3	36	M6
Tom Kelly Rd. 2	49	K11
Tonduff Clo. 12	52	C14
Lugnaquilla Av.		
Tonguefield Rd. 12	48	G12
Tonlegee Av. 5	27	R2
Tonlegee Dr. 5	26	Q2
Tonlegee Rd. 5	26	Q2
Torlogh Gdns. 3	36	M6
Torlogh Par. 3	36	M5
Tourmakeady Rd. 9	24	L3
Tower Av. 6	49	J13
Tower Vw. Cotts. 11	35	J5
Townsend St. 2	44	L9
Trafalgar La., D.L.	59	S15
Trafalgar Ter., D.L.	59	S15
Tram Ter. 3	38	Q7
Tramway Cotts. 7	35	J6
Tramway Ct., Howth	29	W2
Station Rd.		
Tramway Ter. 4	51	O11
Tramway Vills. 6	48	H13
Tranquility Gro. 5	25	O2
Trees Av., Stillorgan	58	P16
Trees Rd., Stillorgan	57	O16
Trevor Ter. 2	44	M9
Greenore Ter.		
Trimleston Av., Booterstown	63	P13
Trimleston Dr., Stillorgan	63	P13
Trimleston Gdns., Stillorgan	63	P13
Trimleston Pk., Stillorgan	63	P13
Trimleston Rd., Stillorgan	63	P13
Trinity Coll. 2	44	L9
Trinity St. 2	43	K9
Trinity Ter. 3	36	M6
Tritonville Av. 4	45	O10
Tritonville Ct. 4	45	O10
Tritonville Cres. 4	45	O10
Tritonville Rd. 4	45	O10
Tryconnell Pk. 8	41	E10
Tucketts La., Howth	31	AA3
Tudor Rd. 6	50	L13
Turnberry, Howth	29	V2
Turrets Flats 6	49	K12
Rathmines Rd. Upper		
Tuscany Downs 5	27	R3
Tuscany Pk., Baldoyle	29	V2
Tymon Castle, Tallaght	52	D15
Tymon La., Tallaght	52	C14
Tymon N. Gdns., Tallaght	52	C15
Tymon N. Grn., Tallaght	52	C15
Tymon N. Gro., Tallaght	52	C15
Tymon N. Lawn, Tallaght	52	C15
Tymon N. Pk., Tallaght	52	C15
Tymon N. Rd., Tallaght	52	C15
Tymonville Av., Tallaght	52	C15
Tymonville Ct., Tallaght	52	C15
Tymonville Cres., Tallaght	52	C15
Tymonville Dr., Tallaght	52	C15
Tymonville Gro., Tallaght	52	C15
Tymonville Pk., Tallaght	52	C15
Tymonville Rd., Tallaght	52	C15
Tyrconnell Rd. 8	41	E10
Tyrconnell St. 8	41	E10
Tyrconnell Vills. 8	41	E9
Grattan Cres.		
Tyrone Pl. 8	41	E10
Tyrone Sq. 8	41	E10
U.S.A. Embassy 8	32	D7
Ulster St. 7	35	J6
Union Pl. (Haroldscross) 6	48	H11
University Coll. 2	43	K10
Upper Cliff Rd., Howth	31	BB3
Upper Glen Rd., Castleknock	32	C7
Uppercross Rd. 8	42	G10
Usher St. 8	43	J9
Ushers Island 8	42	H8
Ushers Quay 8	43	J9
Valentia Par. 7	35	K7
Valentia Rd. 9	24	L4
Valeview Cres. 11	22	G4
Valeview Dr. 11	21	F4
Valeview Gdns. 11	21	F4
Valley Pk. Av. 11	21	E4
Valley Pk. Dr. 11	21	E4
Valley Pk. Rd. 11	21	E4
Vavasour Sq. 4	45	N10
Venetian Hall 5	26	P4
Ventry Dr. 7	34	G5
Ventry Pk. 7	34	G5
Ventry Rd. 7	34	G5
Verbena Av., Kilbarrack	28	U3
Verbena Gro., Kilbarrack	28	U2
Verbena Pk., Kilbarrack	28	U2
Vergemount 6	50	M13
Clonskeagh Rd.		
Vergemount Hall 6	50	M12
Vergemount Isolation Hosp. 6	50	M13
Vergemount Pk. 6	50	M12
Vernon Av. (Clontarf) 3	38	P5
Vernon Av. 6	49	K13
Frankfort Av.		
Vernon Ct. 3	38	Q7
Vernon Dr. 3	38	Q5
Vernon Gdns. 3	38	Q6
Vernon Gro. 3	38	Q6
Vernon Gro. (Rathgar) 6	49	K13
Vernon Par. 3	37	O6
Clontarf Rd.		
Vernon Pk. 3	38	Q6
Vernon Ri. 3	38	Q5
Vernon St. 8	43	J10
Vernon Ter. 6	49	K13
Frankfort Av.		
Veronica Ter. 4	45	N9
Verschoyle Ct. 2	44	M10
Verschoyle Pl.		
Verschoyle Pl. 2	44	M10
Vesey Ms., D.L.	60	U16
Vesey Pl.		
Vesey Pl., D.L.	60	U16
Vesey Ter. (Rathgar) 6	49	J13
Veterinary Laboratory 9	24	M4
Vicar St. 8	43	J9
Victoria Av. 4	50	M12
Victoria Quay 8	42	H8
Victoria Rd. (Clontarf) 3	37	O6
Victoria Rd. (Terenure) 6	55	J14
Victoria St. 8	43	J10
Victoria Ter. 3	38	Q7
Clontarf Rd.		
Victoria Ter. 14	56	M16
Victoria Ter., D.L.	61	V16
Victoria Vills. 3	37	N6
Malahide Rd.		
Victoria Vills. (Rathgar) 6	49	J13

Viking Pl. 7 42 H8
Arbour Hill
Viking Rd. 7 42 H8
Villa Pk. Av. 7 33 F6
Villa Pk. Dr. 33 F6
(Ceide Pairc An Bhailtini) 7
Villa Pk. Gdns. 33 F6
(Gardini Pairc An Bhailtini) 7
Villa Pk. Rd. 33 F6
(Bothar Pairc An Bhailtini) 7
Village, The 5 27 S4
Village, The 9 24 L4
Villarea Pk., D.L. 61 W17
Villiers Rd. 6 49 K13
Vincent St. 8 43 J10
Vincent Ter. 9 35 K5
Violet Hill Dr. 11 22 H4
Violet Hill Pk. 11 22 H4
Violet Hill Rd. 11 22 H4
Virginia Dr. 11 21 F3
Virginia Pk.
Virginia Pk. 11 21 F3

Wad Bri. 9 23 K3
Wadelai Grn. 11 23 K3
Wadelai Rd. 11 23 J3
Wades Av. 5 27 R4
Wainsfort Av. 6 53 F14
Wainsfort Cres. 6 52 F14
Wainsfort Dr. 6 47 F13
Wainsfort Gdns. 6 53 F14
Wainsfort Cres.
Wainsfort Gro. 6 54 G14
Wainsfort Pk. 6 54 G14
Wainsfort Rd. 6 53 F14
Waldemar Ter. 14 56 L16
Waldrons Bri. 14 55 K14
Walk, The 12 53 F15
Walkinstown Av. 12 46 D12
Walkinstown Cres. 12 46 D12
Walkinstown Dr. 12 46 D12
Walkinstown Grn. 12 46 D12
Walkinstown Par. 12 46 D12
Walkinstown Pk. 12 46 D12
Walkinstown Rd. 12 46 D12
Wallace Rd. 12 47 E12
Walnut Av. 9 24 L4
Walnut Ct. 9 24 L4
Walnut Lawn 9 24 L4
Walnut Pk. 9 24 L4
Walnut Ri. 9 24 L4
Walsh Rd. 9 35 K5
Waltham Ter., D.L. 58 Q15
Walworth Rd. 8 43 J10
Victoria St.
Wards Hill 8 43 J10
Warren St. 8 49 K11
Warrenhouse Rd., Baldoyle 29 W2
Warrenmount 8 43 J10
Warrenmount Pl. 8 43 J10
Warrenpoint 3 37 O6
Warrington La. 2 44 M10
Warrington Pl.
Warrington Pl. 2 44 M10
Warwick Ter. 6 50 L11
Sallymount Av.
Wasdale Gro. 6 55 J14
Wasdale Pk. 6 55 J14
Washington La. 14 54 G16
Washington Pk. 14 54 G15
Washington St. 8 43 J10
Waterfall Av. 3 36 L6
Waterfall Rd. 5 27 R4
Waterloo Av. 3 36 M7
Waterloo La. 4 50 L11
Waterloo Rd. 4 50 M11
Watermill Av. 5 27 R4
Watermill Bri. 5 39 S5
Watermill Dr. 5 27 R4
Watermill Lawn 5 27 S4
Watermill Pk. 5 27 R4

Watermill Rd. 27 R4
(Bothan An Easa) 5
Watling St. 8 42 H9
Waverley Av. 3 36 M6
Waverley Ter. 6 49 J12
Kenilworth Rd.
Weavers La. 7 35 J7
Phibsborough Rd.
Weavers Sq. 8 43 J10
Wellesley Pl. 1 36 L7
North Circular Rd.
Wellington Cotts. 12 53 E14
Wellington La. 4 50 M11
Wellington La. 12 53 E14
Wellington 42 G8
Monument 8
Wicklow St.
Wellington Pk. 12 53 E14
Wellington Pl. 50 M11
(Donnybrook) 4
Wellington Pl. N. 7 35 K7
Wellington Quay 2 43 K9
Wellington Rd. 4 50 M11
Wellington Rd. 8 33 F7
Wellington St. 7 35 K7
Wellington St., D.L. 60 U16
Wellmount Av. 11 21 F3
Wellmount Ct. 11 21 F3
Wellmount Cres. 11 21 F3
Wellmount Dr. 11 21 F3
Wellmount Grn. 11 21 F3
Wellmount Par. 11 22 G3
Wellmount Pk. 11 21 F3
Wellmount Rd. 11 21 F3
Wellpark Av. 9 36 L5
Wentworth Ter. 2 44 M9
Hogan Pl.
Werburgh St. 8 43 J9
Wesley Pl. 8 49 J11
Wesley Rd. 6 49 J13
West Oil Jetty 1 62 P9
West Pk. 5 26 Q3
West Pk. Dr. 11 23 J4
West Rd. 3 36 M7
West Ter. 8 41 E9
Westbourne Rd. 6 54 H14
Westbrook Rd. 14 56 L15
Western Rd. 8 42 H10
Western Way 7 35 J7
Westfield Rd. 6 48 H12
Westhampton Pl. 6 48 H13
Terenure Rd. N.
Westland Row 2 44 L9
Westmoreland Pk. 6 50 L11
Westmoreland St. 2 43 K9
Weston Av. 14 56 L16
Weston Clo. 14 56 L16
Weston Gro. 4 56 L16
Weston Pk. 14 56 L16
Weston Rd. 14 56 L16
Westwood Av. 11 21 E3
Westwood Rd. 11 21 E3
Wexford St. 2 43 K10
Wharton Ter. 6 49 J11
Harolds Cross Rd.
White Oak 14 56 M14
Whitebarn Rd. 14 55 K15
Whitebeam Av. 14 50 M13
Whitebeam Rd. 14 50 M13
Whitechurch Abbey 54 H16
14
Whitechurch Rd. 14 54 H16
Whitefriar Pl. 8 43 K9
Aungier St.
Whitefriar St. 43 K9
Whitehall Clo. 12 53 E14
Whitehall Gdns. 12 47 F13
Whitehall Pk. 12 53 E14
Whitehall Rd. 55 K16
(Rathfarnham) 14
Whitehall Rd. E. 12 53 E14
Whitehall Rd. W. 12 53 E14
Whites La. N. 7 35 J7
Whitethorn Av. 5 25 O3
Whitethorn Clo. 5 25 N4
Whitethorn Cres. 5 25 O3

Whitethorn Gro. 5 25 O3
Whitethorn La. 4 45 N9
Thorncastle St.
Whitethorn Pk. 5 25 O3
Whitethorn Ri. 5 25 O4
Whitethorn Rd. 5 25 N3
Whitethorn Rd. 14 50 M13
Whitton Rd. 6 48 H13
Whitworth Av. 3 35 K6
Whitworth Pl.
Whitworth Pl. 3 35 K6
Whitworth Rd. 1 44 M8
Seville Pl.
Whitworth Rd. 9 35 J6
Whitworth Row 1 36 M7
Wicklow La. 2 43 K9
Wicklow St.
Wicklow St. 2 43 K9
Wigan Rd. 9 35 K6
Wilfield 4 51 O11
Wilfrid Rd. 6 49 J12
Willbrook Gro. 14 54 H16
Willbrook St.
Willbrook Lawn 14 54 H16
Willbrook Pk. 14 54 H16
Willbrook Rd. 14 54 H16
Willbrook St. 14 54 H16
Willfield Pk. 4 51 O11
Willfield Rd. 4 51 O11
William St. N. 1 36 L7
William St. S. 2 43 K9
William's La. 1 43 K8
Princes St. N.
William's Pk. 6 49 K11
William's Pl. S. 8 43 J10
William's Pl. Upper 1 35 K6
William's Row 1 43 K8
Willington Av. 12 53 E14
Willington Cres., 53 E15
Tallaght
Willington Dr., 53 E15
Tallaght
Willington Grn. 12 53 E14
Willington Gro. 12 53 E15
Willington Pk. 12 53 E15
Willington Gro.
Willmont Av., D.L. 61 W17
Willow Bk., D.L. 60 U16
Willow Ms. 4 63 P12
Willow Pk. Av. 11 23 J2
Willow Pk. Clo. 11 23 J2
Willow Pk. Cres. 11 22 H2
Willow Pk. Dr. 11 23 J2
Willow Pk. Gro. 11 23 J2
Willow Pk. Lawn 11 23 J2
Willow Pk. Rd. 11 23 J2
Willow Pl., 58 Q14
Booterstown
Willow Ter., D.L. 58 Q14
Rock Rd.
Willowbank Pk. 14 54 G16
Willowfield 4 51 O11
Willowfield Av. 14 57 N15
Willowfield Pk. 14 57 N15
Willows, The 11 34 H5
Willows, The, D.L. 60 T16
Wilson Cres., 57 O15
Stillorgan
Wilson Rd., Stillorgan 57 O15
Wilsons Pl. 2 44 M9
Grants Row
Wilton Pl. 2 44 L10
Wilton Ter. 2 44 L10
Windele Rd. 9 35 K5
Windgate Ri., Howth 31 BB3
Windgate Rd., Howth 31 BB3
Windmill Av. 12 47 F12
Windmill La. 2 44 M9
Windmill Pk. 12 47 F12
Windmill Rd. 12 47 F11
Windsor Av. 3 36 M6
Windsor Ct., D.L. 60 T17
Stradbrook Rd.
Windsor Dr., D.L. 60 T17
Windsor Pk., D.L. 60 T17

Windsor Pl. 2 44 L10
Windsor Rd. 6 49 K12
Windsor Ter. 8 49 J11
Windsor Ter., D.L. 61 V16
Windsor Vills. 3 36 M6
Winetavern St. 8 43 J9
Winton Av. 6 49 J13
Winton Rd. 6 50 L11
Wolfe Tone Av., D.L. 60 U16
Wolfe Tone Quay 7 42 H8
Wolfe Tone St. 1 43 K8
Wolseley St. 8 43 J10
Wood Gro. 14 56 L15
Wood Quay 8 43 J9
Wood St. 8 43 K9
Woodbank Av., 57 O14
Stillorgan
Woodbank Dr. 11 21 E4
Woodbine Av., 57 O14
Stillorgan
Woodbine Clo. 5 27 R3
Woodbine Dr. 5 27 R3
Woodbine Pk. 5 27 R3
Woodbine Pk., 63 P13
Booterstown
Woodbine Rd. 51 O13
(Stillorgan) 4
Woodbine Rd. 5 27 S2
Woodbrook Pk. 14 53 F14
Woodcliff Heights, 31 BB4
Howth
Woodfield Av. 10 41 E9
Woodfield Pl. 10 41 E9
Woodfield Av.
Woodland Pk., 58 P15
Stillorgan
Woodland Vills. 2 50 L11
Woodlands 6 55 J14
Woodlands Av., 58 P16
Stillorgan
Woodlands Dr., 58 P16
Stillorgan
Woodlawn Cres. 14 56 L15
Woodlawn Pk. 14 56 L15
Woodlawn Pk., D.L. 60 U17
Woodlawn Ter. 14 56 L16
Woodside 3 38 Q5
Woodside 14 55 J15
Woodside Dr. 14 55 J15
Woodside Gro. 14 55 J15
Woodstock Gdns. 6 50 L12
Woodview Clo. 5 27 S2
Woodview Cotts. 14 54 H15
Woodview Pk. 5 27 S2
Woodville Rd. 9 35 K5
Botanic Av.
Wynberg Pk., D.L. 59 S16
Wynnefield Rd. 6 49 K12
Wynnsward Dr. 14 56 M14
Wynnsward Pk. 14 56 M14

Xavier Av. 3 36 M7

Yale 14 57 N15
Yankee Ter., 59 R16
Stillorgan
Yellow Rd. 9 24 M4
Yewland Ter. 6 48 H13
York Av. 6 49 K12
York Rd. 4 45 N9
York Rd. 6 49 K12
York Rd., D.L. 60 U16
York St. 2 43 K9
York Ter., D.L. 60 U16

Zion Rd. 6 55 J14
Zoo Rd. 8 42 G8
Zoological Gdns. 8 33 F7